MW01630559

THE DEVELOPMENT OF A PREACHER

The Mentors | The Methodology | The Message

By Dr. Doral R. Pulley

The Development of a Preacher: the Mentors, the Methodology, the Message

ISBN10: 0-9719941-2-9
ISBN13: 978-0-9719941-2-6 (US RETAIL 24.95)

COTEK Press, Publisher
2119 Gwynn Oak Avenue
Woodlawn, Maryland 21207

Printed in the United States of America

THE DEVELOPMENT OF A PREACHER

The Mentors | The Methodology | The Message

WHAT PEOPLE HAVE TO SAY ABOUT
DR. PULLEY AS A PREACHER

"Your ear is to God's mouth."
Overseer Candace Willis

"Bishop, you are just a Word-relayer.
God says it and your relay it to the people."
Min. Kenneth Butler

"You don't understand.
You have life in your mouth.
They only come along like you once in a thousand years."
Dr. Annette Waters

"You are a people-developer.
Through your preaching and teaching you develop people
into what they are called to be."
Elder Pamela Jackson

Dedication | **and Memoriam**

This book is dedicated to the seasoned preachers who helped me to develop into the preacher and Spiritual Leader that I AM today: Evangelist JoAnne Pulley, Pastor Izzelle Crump, Apostle Anne (Smith) Brickhouse and Dr. Bernice Edwell. It is also in memory of the Spiritual Leaders who covered me as a young preacher, opened their pulpits and gave me opportunities to preach, stumble, learn and grow: Bishop Lawrence Thomas, Pastor Elizabeth Thompson, Dr. Joseph M. Showell and Bishop Horace O. Ward.

I AM grateful for my life-long friend, Elder Ann Taylor, Spiritual Leader of A.L.I.V. Ministries in Fayetteville, North Carolina and the members of my class who were the catalyst for this book. They put a demand on the anointing, the God in me, and this is the product.

I appreciate all of the preachers that I have trained over the years through Mind of Christ School of Ministry's courses, Sermon Preparation and Advanced Sermon Preparation. Each of you have helped me perfect this model and were a platform for me to tell my story, The Development of a Preacher.

TABLE OF CONTENTS

INTRODUCTION

Most of my development as a preacher took place during my formative years between the ages of 7-18. By the time that I was 18 years old, my preaching style had been established. I founded the Church of the Everlasting Kingdom, Inc (COTEK) and became the Spiritual Leader of COTEK at 19 years old. As I continued to preach as a Spiritual Leader and a bishop, my preaching was perfected.

Early on, I learned that God had a message that God desired me as a messenger to convey to the masses. Mentors taught me that a preacher was a messenger and that good preaching begins in prayer. Therefore, before I prepare a message, it is imperative that I pray and ask God: "what message did you desire for me to give to your particular people at this time?" It is just as important that I sit in the stillness and the silence to hear what the Spirit is saying.

A message is different from a sermon. Sermons are more universal and can be given to anyone at any time. A preacher can have a good sermon but a poor message. The hermeneutics and homiletics may be in order but if it is not the specific message that God desires to convey to a group of people at a particular time then it is ineffective.

People need to hear from God. A preacher is a conduit through which the Holy Spirit channels the right and perfect message to a specific people. Sometimes a message is a confirmation to something that they have already heard, and they need to added assurance that they are making the right decisions about a matter. Other times a message is a "Wake Up Call" to those who are spiritually asleep and have not awakened to hear God's Word or God's will for their lives.

The purpose of this book is to educate, empower and encourage those who are beginning their preaching ministry or those who have never been formally trained in preaching.

This is a workbook designed as a developmental tool for preachers.

Each chapter has 5 dimensions:

I. An anecdote about my preaching experience at a particular age
II. One of Pulley's Preaching Principle that I learned from the experience
III. A scripture that supports the preaching principle
IV. A Historic quote from one of the preaching giants that helped develop me as a preacher
V. A Historic message (more than 20 years old) that I have preached and received feedback about.

There are different types of messages and the type of message is identified as:

- **Expository** – a message based on the unfolding or explaining of a passage of scripture that is not a story. Psalms 91 is an example.

- **Textual** – a shorter expository message. Instead of the message covering an entire passage, the message focuses on a few verses. Psalms 91:1-2 is an example.

- **Topical** – a message based on a scriptural subject such as joy. The preacher then researches and brings together related scriptures on that subject (Nehemiah 8:10, Psalm 16:11, Isaiah 12:3, John 15:11, I Peter 1:8).

- **Biographical** – a message that is based on the life of a biblical figure such as Joseph. The points of the message are based on different scriptural instances of the person's life (Genesis 37-50).

- **Narrative** – a message that is based on an entire story in the Bible such as the birth of Jesus (Matthew 1-2, Luke 1-2).

- **Historical Incident** - a shorter narrative message that is based on a part of the story such as the exchange between Mary and Elizabeth (Luke 1:36-56).

There are also exercises at the end of each chapter to help the reader reflect and grow as a preacher such as:

- Completing an evaluation form for a message.

- Developing the outline of the message in the chapter and making it your own.

- Reading the message in the chapter and creating a different message.

- Retitling the message.

- Developing a message out of the title that is given.

CHAPTER ONE

THE CALL of a Preacher

(Age 7)

"You Must Be Called To Preach!"
Bishop Lawrence Thomas

"Brethren, give all diligence to make your calling and election sure."
II Peter 1:10

Chapter One—The CALL of a Preacher

As a child, I loved going to church. I felt most at home in church. At the age of 3, I became aware of the Holy Spirit in an old-fashioned Pentecostal service at a church next door to our house, New Galilee Church of God in Christ Jesus under the auspices of Bishop Mileage Golphin.

As a youth, my parents were not into church. Although they were both raised in church, as they grew older, they strayed. My mom and her best friend, JoAnn (Auntie Anne) dated brothers. Auntie Anne and Uncle George got into church and got married. Auntie Anne became an evangelist and Uncle George became a deacon. My parents, Renee' and Beannie, never married and did not get back into church until much later in their lives. Therefore, as a child, if I wanted to go to church, I had to spend the weekend with Auntie Anne and Uncle George. Together, Auntie Anne and Uncle George had five children. Although I was an only child, I fit right in with my cousins as if I was just another one of the children.

As an evangelist, Auntie Anne traveled to various churches spreading the good news wherever, whenever and however she could. One of the churches that she joined was Rock of Ages Pentecostal Church under the leadership of Bishop Lawrence Thomas. We were very active in the church especially in the Youth Department. Everyone remarked about how well-mannered, well-groomed and well-behaved the Pulley children were.

The second Sunday in June every year was Children's Day. It was like a second Easter where children would dress up and play various parts in the worship service. The Saturday before Children's Day in 1978, I was 7 years old and we were at church practicing our parts for the Big Children Day's Service the next day. It was going to be the biggest Children's Day ever because several churches from the Baltimore-Washington metropolitan area were coming together to celebrate this auspicious occasion.

While at practice, Elder Lynn Thomas who was my Sunday School Teacher, the president of the Youth Department and the pastor's daughter-in-law, received a telephone call that pulled her away from the rehearsal. When she came back to the rehearsal, she was sad. We asked her what was wrong and she said that the preacher for tomorrow's service was not going to be able to make it. She then asked if any of us wanted to speak or wanted to say anything to fill in the time. All of the youth from ages 5-18 declined. When I saw that everyone else had said, "No!" I raised my hand and said, "Yes, I will do it!"

Elder Lynn was so excited. I told my Auntie Anne what happened and she said that she would help me prepare my message. We decided that I would preach from Luke 15:11-33 about the Prodigal Son and we entitled the message, "Are you lost?" What a perfect title. I felt like I was lost. I had no clue what I was doing or what I was getting myself into. It seemed like we were working on the message all night long. While the other children were outside playing ball, I was in the house with my aunt working on my message. I was nervous and excited all at the same time. I called my parents and all of my family to ask them to come to church that Sunday afternoon to hear me preach.

The children were beautiful and the service was Spirit-filled. Elder Lynn introduced me and told the story of how I became the preacher for the service. I was so scared. I was so short that I had to stand on a milk crate so that people could see me from the podium. Nevertheless, once I got the microphone in my hand the fear left and the Spirit fell upon me and spoke through me. After that service, many of the youth leaders from the various churches invited me to come to their churches to preach for their annual or monthly Youth Service. Before I could respond Bishop Thomas stepped in and told Elder Lynn to take their information and we would get back with them.

Bishop Thomas pulled me into his study and said, "Son, you did a great job. We are so proud of you. But we have to make sure that you are really called to preach. We have to be sure that this was not just a one-time thing." Bishop Thomas said that he would talk to my mother and see if we could fast and pray to be sure that God was calling me to preach. After being convinced by my Auntie Anne, my mom agreed and we fasted and prayed that week.

When Bishop Thomas and I met the next Sunday, we were both convinced that God had called me to preach. Bishop Thomas told me that I answered my call much like the Prophet Isaiah. "Also I heard the voice of the Lord, saying, whom shall I send, and who will go for us? Then said I, Here am I; send me (Isaiah 6:8)." Given the opportunity to preach, I made myself available, prepared and people were blessed by the message.

Elder Lynn called the youth leaders from the various churches back and my calendar was filled with preaching engagements throughout Baltimore, Washington and Virginia. Immediately, my life took a different course. I knew that not only was I called but I was chosen because I answered the call. "Many are called, but few are chosen (Matthew 22:14)."

The Call Narrative makes you sure

Every preacher has a call narrative: a particular day, time and circumstance under which he knows that he is the messenger of God. Within the Call Narrative and the events surrounding it are also prophetic indicators about the preacher's specific call including target audience, future goals and aspirations, ministry gifts, etc. Every call narrative is unique to the messenger. It doesn't have to be a great outward sign like a bright light or a voice from heaven for a person to know that she is called. It can be as simple as an internal knowing that is confirmed by other people. God always confirms the call through others. Others will bear witness of the call on our lives. No matter how the call narrative takes place; the most important thing is that the messenger knows that he is called by God to preach.

God is calling all of us to some form of ministry. The word, minister, means to serve. God has given each of us at least one talent that can be used to serve God and others. We just have to discover what that talent is. Everyone is called to share their testimony with others and tell others the good news. However, that does not mean that everyone is called to preach in a formal manner.

The Call Narrative gives the preacher something to refer back to during times of trial and tribulation. When things in ministry are not going the way that we expected them to go, we can always rest in the assurance that **I know that God called me to preach**. We can also have peace in the fact that we know that we are doing what God has called us to do. Regardless of the results of our preaching ministry, we know that we will be blessed for our obedience.

Questions for Reflection

1. How was the call of the young preacher confirmed?

2. What can we predict about the young preacher's destiny as a result of the elements of his call narrative?

3. Based on the call story you just read. Write your own call story.

4. Outside of your personal encounter with God, what other evidence is there that you are called to preach?

Message #1

Sermon Title: Are You Lost? Luke 15:11-33

Sermon Type: Narrative

I. Introduction - Missing Children, "It's 10:00 pm! Do you know where your children are?"

II. The Prodigal Son was lost in the world.

III. The Father was lost without his son.

IV. The Older Brother was lost in the house because he did not know the benefits of sonship.

V. Conclusion – Which one of characters in the story do you represent?

How are you lost?

You can be found if you want to be found.

- *The prodigal son was found. He found his way back home.*
- *The Father was found. He found his joy. He was rejoicing because of his son's return home.*
- *The Older brother was found. He found the benefits sonship.*

Exercise

1. Read the text 3 times.

2. Further develop this message outline with more details. Make sure that every Roman numeral has an A, B and C.

3. Give the message a different title. Be creative.

4. Give the message a different introduction. Make it relevant today.

5. Give the message a different conclusion. Make it your own.

6. Describe a time in your life when you felt lost.

7. Which character in the story do you resonate most with? Why?

8. Which character in the story do you resonate least with? Why?

CHAPTER TWO

THE PROTECTION of a Preacher

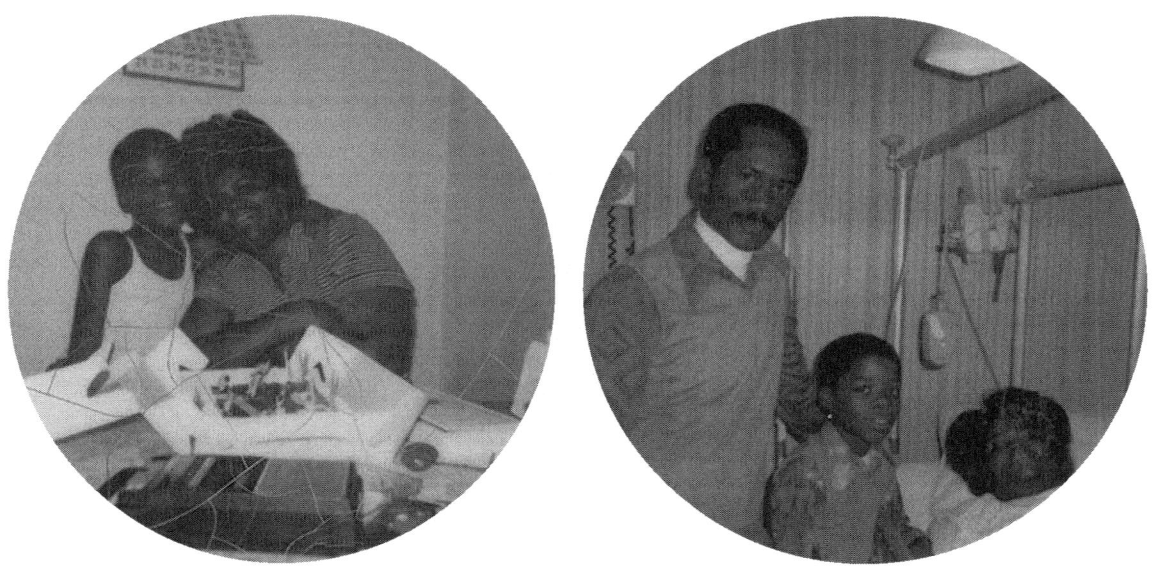

(Age 8)

"Preaching Saved Your Life"

Evangelist JoAnn Pulley

*1 He that dwells in the secret place of the most High shall abide under the shadow of the
Almighty. 2 I will say of the Lord, He is my refuge and my fortress: my God; in him will I
trust. 3 Surely he shall deliver thee from the snare of the fowler, and from the noisome pestilence. 4 He shall cover thee with his feathers, and under his wings shalt thou trust: his
truth shall be thy shield and buckler. 5 Thou shalt not be afraid for the terror by night; nor
for the arrow that flies by day; 6 Nor for the pestilence that walks in darkness; nor for the
destruction that wastes at noonday. 7 A thousand shall fall at thy side, and ten thousand at
thy right hand; but it shall not come nigh thee. 8 Only with thine eyes shalt thou behold and
see the reward of the wicked. 9 Because thou hast made the Lord, which is my refuge, even
the most High, thy habitation; 10 There shall no evil befall thee, neither shall any plague
come nigh thy dwelling. 11 For he shall give his angels charge over thee, to keep thee in all
thy ways. 12 They shall bear thee up in their hands, lest thou dash thy foot against a stone.
13 Thou shalt tread upon the lion and adder: the young lion and the dragon shalt thou
trample under feet. 14 Because he hath set his love upon me, therefore will I deliver him: I
will set him on high, because he hath known my name. 15 He shall call upon me, and I will
answer him: I will be with him in trouble; I will deliver him, and honor him. 16 With long life
will I satisfy him, and show him my salvation.* Psalm 91:1-16

Chapter Two—The PROTECTION of a Preacher

At 8 years old, six months after I accepted my call to preach and began preaching throughout the Baltimore-Washington metropolitan area, my family (me, my mom and my stepfather) was involved in a tragic electrical fire. We lived on the third floor of the DuPont Apartments in the Park Heights area of Baltimore City. The only exit out of the fire was through our third-story bedroom window. My stepfather tied sheets around the bed post enough to make a "rope" stretching to the second floor. He told us that once the rope ran out that we had to let go and jump to the ground. My mother jumped and she became paralyzed from her waist down. My stepfather jumped and broke his leg and his hip. I jumped and did not get a scratch.

When my mother got settled in the hospital, she kept asking "where are the little children who caught Doral? I want to give them something for saving his life." The residents of the apartment building told her that there were no little children outside at 8 o'clock at night which was the time of the fire. My mom maintained that as she was lying on the ground and watching me jump from the window that she saw little children dressed in white who caught me. I did not see the little children but I did have a feeling of being caught and let down to the ground. I was so concerned about my mom that I did not really focus on how I jumped out of the same window unharmed.

While my mom was in the hospital for nine months and enduring 13 operations, I stayed with Auntie Anne and Uncle George. It was home to me because I was used to being there on the weekends, going to church with them and playing with my cousins who had become like brothers and sisters to me. My second home, their house, became my primary residence. I transferred schools and we transferred churches but I kept preaching.

One Sunday afternoon after I finished preaching the message, "Things Go Better with Jesus," at Christian Temple Faith Church, Auntie Anne said she wanted to talk to me. After dinner, Auntie Anne asked me, "Do you know who you are? Do you understand why you were not hurt in the fire?" I told her that I did not really understand. I only knew what my mom told me about the little children dressed in white who caught me. Auntie Anne explained to me that I was a preacher, God's special messenger, and that I had a message for the masses. She told me that I would always be protected because I was the messenger and the message was inside of me. Auntie Anne further clarified that the little children dressed in white were angels. She looked me in my eyes and told me, "Preaching saved your life. God dispatched angels to catch you because you are his little preacher boy." She read to me Psalms 91, we prayed together and I went to bed.

The Preacher is Divinely Protected

As a preacher, you are God's vessel. The anointing of God flows through you. Not only does the oil flow through you to bless other people but you contain the oil and the oil blesses and protects you as well. In addition to being God's vessel, you are God's oracle, God's mouthpiece. "If any man speak, let him speak as the oracles of God; if any man minister, let him do it as of the ability which God gives: that God in all things may be glorified through Jesus Christ, to whom be praise and dominion for ever and ever. Amen. (I Peter 4:11)." As an oracle of God, you are divinely protected so that you can say what God has called you to say, do what God has called you to do and go where God has called you to go.

Some preachers assert that accepting the call "in and of itself" spared their lives. Due to their acceptance of the call, they made different choices than they would have had they not accepted the call. Because of their acceptance and respect for their call, they observed certain limits and boundaries related to sex, alcohol, drugs and gambling. They believe that they were spared from disease, overdose, etc. because they were walking worthy of the vocation for which they were called (Ephesians 4:1).

In addition to being protected as a result of accepting the call, other preachers attest that their lives were spared prior to accepting their call to salvation and their subsequent call to preach. They boldly proclaim that although they were in the same places where their friends were shot and killed that they were protected. They maintain that God protected them from danger because "there was a call on their lives" that God knew they would accept. "Whom he did foreknow, he also did predestinate and those whom he predestinated them he also called... (Romans 8:29-30)."

Divine Protection Affirmation

I AM divinely protected by God. I honor, fear, reverence and respect the Lord. Therefore, the angels of the Lord are encamped about me. There is a hedge of protection around me, my marriage, my family and all of our possessions. Anything that gets through that hedge of protection and gets to us was meant to be for God's glory and for our good.

Questions for Reflection

1. Since you accepted your call to preach, describe a situation in your life where you knew that you were protected by God.

2. Describe a time in your life where you made different choices because you accepted your call to preach.

3. Do you remember a time in your life prior to salvation and accepting the call where you were divinely protected by God? If so, describe the situation where you experienced divine protection.

4. Repeat the Divine Protection Affirmation every day at least once a day for the next week.

5. Journal in the space provided below about how you feel each time after repeating the affirmation.

Message #2

Sermon Title: Things Go Better with Jesus. Romans 8:28

Sermon Type: Biographical/Textual

I. Introduction – There are things in life that go together (Peanut Butter & Jelly, Eggs & Bacon, Broccoli & Cheese)

II. Sickness + Jesus = Healing – Example: Jesus healed Peter's mother-in-law who was sick of fever (Matthew 8:14-17).

III. Lack + Jesus = Miracle – Example: Peter getting the money out of the fish's mouth (Matthew 17:24-27).

IV. Death + Jesus = Resurrection – Example: Peter was there when Jesus raised Jarius' daughter from the dead (Mark 5:21-24, 35-43).

V. Conclusion – It does not matter what you mix with Jesus, it's going to turn out right. If you don't mix the thing with Jesus, then it won't turn out right.

Exercise

1. In order to properly interpret a text, a preacher has to answer various questions. Answer the following questions about Romans 8:28:

   Who is speaking?

   What is being said?

   When is it being said?

   Where is it written and where does the story take place?

   Why is this being said (what events and activities surround the text)?

   How does this text apply to my life?

2. Choose one of the Gospel texts in the outline and answer the questions above.

3. Using the introduction as an example, give 10 other items that are normally coupled together.
   a.
   b.
   c.
   d.
   e.
   f.
   g.
   h.
   i.
   j.

4. List 2 other biblical examples of life situations where "Things that go better with Jesus."

5. In the space provided below, write about a personal example of something that went better as a result of Jesus Christ being in your life.

CHAPTER THREE

THE Preacher's STUDY

(Age 9)

"You Must Know that Bible."
Pastor Izzelle Crump

Study to show yourself approved unto God, a worker who needs not to be ashamed, rightly dividing the Bible of truth.
II Timothy 2:15

Chapter Three—The Preacher's STUDY

At 9 years old, I was a cute little boy who was talking loud and saying nothing. People in the audience were not really paying attention to what I was saying. They were just mesmerized by the fact that I, a 9 year old little black boy, was saying it. The congregants often commented, "Oh, isn't he so cute." Other parishioners would remark, "Child, can you believe he's only 9 years old?" My father said, "Doral is young. This preaching thing is a phase. He will grow out of it." However, I didn't feel like it was phase that I was going through. I felt like it was a life-long calling that I had to fulfill. I did not want to let God down.

After preaching for two years, the novelty of preaching and being a preacher wore off. The popularity and the speaker's offerings were insufficient for me. I did not want that "phase thing" that my father said to be true. I really believed that God had called me to preach. I prayed and asked God, "How can I get people to actually listen to what I have to say? How can I get people to pay attention to the message that I am trying to get across?" God did not answer but Pastor Crump certainly did.

Pastor Crump, the pastor of Christian Temple Faith Church, told me that a preacher only has two things that make people listen to him: his testimony and his knowledge of the Bible. He further explained that since I did not have much of a testimony such as deliverance from this or that (alcohol, sex, drugs, prison, miraculous healing) or general life experience (marriage, family, job, community, finances, etc.) that "you must know that Bible."

Since I didn't know the Bible like most preachers, Pastor Crump agreed to give me weekly Bible lessons and help me develop my messages. One of the messages that we worked on for a few weeks was "If God is dead." I preached that message a few times until I knew it like I knew my name. My mother invested in my ministry and she gave Pastor Crump a love offering for the one-on-one weekly Bible studies. Much like parents pay for their children to have private piano lessons, my mother paid for me to get personal Bible knowledge.

In addition to private lessons, Pastor Crump suggested that I read and study the Bible every day. He also recommended that I fully participate in Sunday School and the weekly Bible Class during the week. I had a lot on my plate as a youngster. I had to go to school and get good grades. I had to do my house chores. I had to help my mother who was paralyzed in the wheelchair as a result of the fire. Sometimes when the Home Health Care Assistant wasn't able to make it or my step-father wasn't home from work, I had to empty my mom's bed pan, discard her sanitary napkins and get dinner started. Pastor Crump added all of the Bible learning to my already packed plate. I did not mind because I knew that God called me to be a preacher.

My great-grandmother, Beatrice Martin, did not attend church much when I was developing as a preaching. Neither was she supportive of me being a preacher at such a young age. She never came to hear me preach. Nevertheless, when I was 9 years old, she gave me a clock with a gold plaque called the Preacher's Study. On the plaque, it emphasized that "it is not the Preacher's Office but the Preacher's Study. Preachers are supposed to study." Even though I was too young to have my own study, I hung the clock/plaque over my desk in my room. I designated that space as my study area and prayed that one day God would give me a Study and a library filled with books that would help me be a better preacher.

The Bible is our manual

The Bible is more than just one book. It is a compilation of 66 books. Due to the historical nature of the scriptures, they must be read, studied and researched. The Old Testament lays a foundation for the New Testament. The original languages of the scriptures are Hebrew, Greek and Aramaic. The King James Version that we hold so dear is a translation from these languages to Latin and to English. The Bible that we read today is "not the inspired Word" but a translation of the Bible received into a language that we can understand. Therefore, we can use any of the translations of the scriptures as long as the original meaning is preserved.

Also, many accounts of scripture are paralleled with other scriptures; therefore, scripture should be compared with scripture. To get the full understanding of the scriptures, it is important to study the history and context of the scriptures. "And Jesus answering said unto them, Do ye not therefore err, because ye know not the scriptures, neither the power of God (Mark 12:24)?" The scriptures are often misunderstood and taken out of context. These misinterpretations have caused confusion, dissention and many people have been put into unnecessary bondage. Here are some helpful hints that will assist you in interpreting scripture properly. Never isolate a verse of scripture; always put it in the context of the chapter and the book in which it is found. Whenever you read a passage, ask the following questions: Whose speaking? To whom is the author speaking? Why is this being said? How does this verse apply to my life?

The Bible is central to the life of every preacher. Jesus said, "if ye continue in my Word, then are ye my disciples indeed (John 8:31)." The only way that we can follow Christ correctly is by practicing the principles of the Bible. Reading the Word is simply opening up the Bible and reading it. We must read the Bible everyday even if it is no more than a verse of scripture daily. The Bible is our guideline and the reference point for everything that we do. When all else fails, we can rely on the Bible to give us clear direction and instruction. The

Bible is one of our major weapons against the kingdom of darkness. In order to defeat negativity, we must read the Bible.

Reading is just the beginning. After we read the Bible, we must study the Word to understand its full meaning and application to our lives. Attending Bible Study, Sunday School Classes, School of Ministry and Seminary courses are excellent resources in helping us study God's Word more fully.

Jesus and the scriptures

The foundation of the written scriptures is the oral tradition. Once the oral tradition was put into written form, it became a part of the worship experience for Jews. Jesus Christ was a person who attended corporate worship regularly and he participated in the services. In Luke 4:18-19, Jesus Christ is on the program to read the scriptures.

> *"And when he had opened the book, he found the place where it was written, The Spirit of the Lord is upon me, because he hath anointed me to preach the gospel to the poor; he hath sent me to heal the brokenhearted, to preach deliverance to the captives, and recovering of sight to the blind, to set at liberty them that are bruised, To preach the acceptable year of the Lord. And he closed the book, and he gave it again to the minister, and sat down."*

As preachers of Christ, we are not to take for granted scripture reading as a part of the order of worship. It is a vital part of the service and it is an honor to be asked to read the scriptures.

> *"And he began to say unto them, This day is this scripture fulfilled in your ears (Luke 4:21)."*

Hearing, reading and studying the Bible is just a beginning. We must also take what we have heard and read and apply it to our lives. In our text, Jesus Christ not only read the scriptures but he applied the scriptures to himself. He made a connection with the written scriptures and made it the living Word. The Bible is not just facts, stories and information. It is filled with principles that can empower us to lead holistically healthy, balanced and well-rounded lives if we apply it to our lives.

> *Think not that I am come to destroy the law, or the prophets: I am not come to destroy, but to fulfill (Matthew 5:17).*

During Jesus Christ's earthly ministry, he established his kingdom which often appeared to contradict Jewish teachings such as: stoning people who were caught in adultery, eating with unwashed hands, eating with sinners and healing on the Sabbath. In our text, Jesus Christ clarified his mission and his purpose. He did not come to destroy or discredit the Law.

He came to fulfill the Law. "Fulfilling the Law" means bringing out the true intention of the Author. Because Jesus Christ knew the Father/Author intimately, he could provide a better understanding of what God meant by what He said. We follow Jesus Christ's view of scripture and regard it with the same dignity and openness that he did.

For verily I say unto you, Till heaven and earth pass, one jot or one tittle shall in no wise pass from the law, till all be fulfilled (Matthew 5:18).

The scriptures are not fairy tales. All of the prophecies of the scripture from Genesis to Revelation have been or will be fulfilled. God watches over his word to perform it. God is not a liar. If God said it, then he is going to do it. If God spoke it, then he will bring it to pass. This also gives every preacher the assurance that whatever word God has spoken over their lives will come to pass. No matter how long it takes. God is faithful and every prophecy we have received through the mouth of his prophets will happen. The practices of the scriptures may change but the principles remain the same. We, too, are called not just to preach the scriptures but to fulfill the scriptures.

Preachers, there is so much to study!

The preacher has to be a Bible student who is always in the posture of learning and growing. "But grow in grace and in the knowledge of our Lord and Savior Jesus Christ (II Peter 3:18)." No matter how much we know about the scriptures, there is always so much more to learn. Preaching is our profession and the Bible is our manual. Therefore, preachers should always be engaged in some type of biblical study and research whether it is formal (Bible School, School of Ministry, Seminary) or informal (Personal Bible Study, Church Bible Class, Sunday School, Vacation Bible School).

In addition to studying the Bible, preachers must pay close attention to the life of Jesus Christ, who is our Wayshower and example of what it means to be fully human and fully divine. Jesus Christ was the greatest preacher who ever lived and he commanded us to "take my yoke upon you, and learn of me; for I am meek and lowly in heart: and you shall find rest unto your souls (Matthew 11:29)." Although it is important to study the treasured theologians of history and to listen to the prolific preachers of our day, we must not lose sight of our call to pattern our lives and ministries after Jesus Christ.

In order to be a preacher, we must understand the person whom we are following. The scriptures provide us with a basic knowledge of who Jesus Christ is. Through the scriptures we learn about his birth, life, ministry, death, burial, resurrection, ascension and second coming. Only after we receive a foundational understanding of who Christ is through the scripture can we develop a personal relationship with him. The more we walk with Christ and have various life experiences the more that we will learn about him. No one can take away from us the knowledge that we have received through intimacy with him.

Paul, an apostle of Jesus Christ, instructed his son in the gospel, Timothy, to study and pay close attention to himself. "Take heed to yourself, and unto the doctrine; continue in them: for in doing this you will both save yourself and them that hear you (I Timothy 4:16)." In addition to studying the Bible and the life of Jesus Christ, we must learn from our experiences and not repeat past mistakes. We can only do this by taking time to study ourselves. God is speaking to us and giving us messages through our experiences if we just pay attention. There are messages that we are preaching through our daily lives. We are living epistles (II Corinthians 3:2). We are the Bible made flesh today (John 1:1, 14).

As preachers, not only must we study the Bible, the life of Jesus Christ and ourselves, we must study the world around us. God is also speaking to us and giving us messages through current events. Preachers must have some medium to stay in touch with what's going on in the world in which we live. We can get the news through radio, television, newspaper, magazines or even electronically so that we can preach the good news in a relevant and effective manner. When we are aware of the issues of our day, we can make proper biblical applications so that our parishioners are equipped to handle these stressors.

Preachers must know how they see it!

The two major groups within Christianity are Catholics and Protestants. The Catholic Bible has 73 books and the Protestant Bible has only 66 books in its canon. Although Protestants use the same Bible, there are so many denominations within Protestantism. Each denomination has its own beliefs, doctrines and dogma based upon its interpretations of scripture and traditions.

Although the Bible is the preacher's primary text, the preacher has to pick a point of view or a way of looking at scripture. How the preacher looks at the Bible determines how he or she will interpret it. It's like looking at the world through "rose colored glasses." If the person has on rose-colored glasses, then he or she will see everything rosy.

Some of the primary ways to view scripture are:

1. **Literal** – People who view the Bible literally believe that the Bible is the inherent infallible Word of God; therefore, nothing should be added to it or taken away from it. They believe that the Bible means exactly what it says and says exactly what it means; therefore, people should do exactly what it says, literally.
2. **Analytical** – People who view the Bible analytically believe that the history, culture and language in which the scriptures were written must be considered to give proper context and interpretation of the text. They believe that the Bible is

literature; therefore, literary criticism is necessary.

3. **Metaphysical** – People who view the Bible metaphysically believe that the most important aspect of scripture is life application. People with this point of view avoid debates about scripture because they see the scriptures as having multiple meanings; therefore, each person should pray and gain the understanding that he or she needs to live their best lives and to be their best selves.

Most preachers are not limited to one particular view of scripture. Some view the scriptures differently based on what division of the Bible they are reading (Old Testament, New Testament). Others have a general combined view of scripture such as Analytical/Metaphysical or Literal/Analytical. Regardless of what the view is, the preacher has to be aware of how they are looking at scripture so that they know how they are arriving at various conclusions.

Questions for Reflection

1. Do you have a designated study area? If so, where is it? If not, why not?
2. Describe your current informal biblical course of study.
3. Describe your current formal biblical course of study.
4. In what ways are you emulating the life and ministry of Jesus Christ?
5. List 5 of the latest lessons that you are learning about yourself.
   a.
   b.
   c.
   d.
   e.

Questions of Reflection (continued)

6. How do you stay abreast of current events taking place in your community and in the world in general?

7. Who is your favorite historic theologian? Explain.

8. Who is your favorite modern-day preacher? Explain.

9. List the books that you are currently reading.

10. What books do you desire to add to your library?

11. List and explain in your own words, the three primary views of scripture.

12. How do you view scripture? How do you use this view in developing your messages?

Message #3

Sermon Title: If God is Dead... Matthew 22:31-33

Sermon Type: Textual

I. Introduction – Song – "If God is dead...what makes my life worth living? I'm glad I know He lives..."

II. God is alive in nature (flowers, trees, sunshine, rain, etc.)

III. God is alive in animals (birds, dogs, cats, etc.)

IV. God is alive in us (The breath of God).

V. Conclusion – Song – "God's not dead. He is yet alive. I can feel him in my hands. I can feel him in my feet. I can feel him all over me."

Exercise

1. Give scriptural references to validate the point, God is alive in nature.
2. Give scriptural references to validate the point, God is alive in animals.
3. Give scriptural references to validate the point, God is alive in human beings.
4. What do you think about the song used for the Introduction?
5. What do you think about the song used for the Conclusion?
6. Have you used a song in an Introduction to one of your messages? Why or why not?
7. Have you used a song in a Conclusion to one of your messages? Why or why not?

CHAPTER FOUR

THE Preacher's SERVICE

(Age 10)

"Preaching is not just in the pulpit."
Pastor Elizabeth Thompson

But he that is greatest among you shall be your servant. And whosoever shall exalt himself shall be abased; and he that shall humble himself shall be exalted.
Matthew 23:11-12

Chapter Four—The Preacher's SERVICE

At 10 years old, I was alone at Rock of Ages. Auntie Anne and her family left the church to be a part of another local assembly. When my family left the church, I stayed at the church because it was around the corner from my house. Once my mother was released from the hospital and rehabilitation, my immediate family (me, mom and my stepfather) moved to Seton Apartments, an apartment complex, which was right behind the church. I could walk to Bible Study, Sunday School and Worship Services. I no longer had to stay at my aunt's house for the weekend if I wanted to go to church.

While at Rock of Ages, I became close with another family in the church, the Ellison family. Sister Janice Ellison was the choir director for the Male Chorus that I joined. I got really close to the family when Sister Ellison asked me to lead the song, "I had a talk with God last night." They took me into their hearts and their home. Sister Ellison asked my mother could she be my godmother and my mom agreed.

One Sunday morning at Rock of Ages, there was a physical altercation among the leadership of the church. As a result of this fight, a lot of people left the church and went into different directions. The Ellison Family was one of the families that left the church and I eventually stopped going to church.

At such a young age, I was so hurt and disappointed in the leadership of the church that I did not want anything to do with church anymore. People called me and offered to take me to different churches but I did not want to go. I called myself backsliding. This backsliding season was really a developmental phase where I realized that I was 10 years old like all of the rest of children in my apartment complex. For about 3 months, I stopped going to church and I experimented with all of the secular things the children my age were doing: sex, alcohol, marijuana, listening to disco music and going to "Disco Skate."

I soon grew weary of backsliding. I missed being in church. I missed preaching. I felt out of place. I felt lost like the prodigal son from my initial sermon. One day Sister Ellison called me and invited me to go to her new church, the Holy Name Church of Jesus under the auspices of Pastor Elizabeth Thompson. The church was on the other side of town but the church van picked me up.

When I first met Pastor Thompson, I was afraid of her. Although I enjoyed her preaching and teaching, she seemed like a mean old lady. After attending the church a few times, I requested to meet with her about my ministry. I wanted Pastor Thompson to know that I was a preacher and that I was ready to start preaching again. Preaching for me was like breathing. If I could not preach, then I felt like I could not breathe.

Pastor Thompson started the meeting with, "I don't think you are a cute little boy preacher." I told her that God had given me a message to preach and I had to preach it. The message was entitled, **"They've Got Some Wicked Ways but They Are Still My People** (II Chronicles 7:14)." She told me, "Preach it over the toilet bowl because the men's bathroom needed to be cleaned. Maybe Mr. Toilet bowl will listen to what you have to say." I told her that I was not a janitor but I was a preacher. She told me in no uncertain terms that I was not ready to preach in her church until I was ready to serve. Pastor Thompson explained to me, "Preaching is not just in the pulpit."

I stopped going to Holy Name Church of Jesus for about a month because I did not like what Pastor Thompson said to me. I felt like she did not understand my call to preach. Nevertheless, there was something about what she said that resonated with me. My spirit accepted her words as truth. I started going back to the church and I found out who was in charge of cleaning the church, Brother Kilpatrick. I asked Brother Kilpatrick could I help him clean the men's room. He was shocked but he showed me how to clean it and what supplies to use. Eventually, I learned to preach my sermons while cleaning the bathroom and Bro. Toilet Bowl became my "Amen Corner."

Serving in the Church Outside of the Pulpit

In addition to cleaning the church, I learned to serve on various auxiliaries of the church and in various capacities in the local assembly: Youth and Young Adult Ministry, Brotherhood Chorus, Youth Choir Director, Church Historian, Pastor's Aide Committee, Radio and Television Choir and the Missionary Board. I started seeing church and ministry in a whole different light. I started seeing the preacher as the person in the church who did "whatever his hands found to do (Ecclesiastes 9:10)." I realized that not only had God given the preacher a mouth and voice but God had also given the preacher hands and feet that needed to be used.

After serving outside of the pulpit for about six months, Pastor Thompson requested to meet with me. I was so excited. I thought that she was going to put me on the preaching rotation. Boy was I wrong. She told me before I began preaching that I had to learn more about the Bible and that I had to learn how to teach. She felt that teaching Sunday School was just the way to do it. Pastor Thompson called the Sunday School Superintendent, Elder Henry Davis, into to the meeting and told him to make me a Sunday School Teacher. Elder Davis assigned me to the Primary Class which was ages 6-8. He gave me a teacher's manual and a student copy of the book and the next Sunday I was teaching.

I was a little nervous. When I shared my anxiety with my mother, she told me that my Sunday School students were no different than my cousins with whom I used to play church.

She told me to see my Sunday School students like the children in the neighborhood that I made sit on the steps and listen to me preach. Although my mother was not into church at the time, it seemed like she always knew just what to say to help me in my ministry. Her words made me extremely comfortable and I began to enjoy teaching. I was having fun learning more about the Bible and sharing what I learned with my students. My students listened to me and I had very few disciplinary issues. I was proud of my students especially during Review Time when my students shared what they learned with the entire congregation. My class won several awards for having the Best Attendance and the Highest Offering.

Sister Anne Jackson, the Director of Vacation Bible School, asked me to teach in the summer. She gave me the Junior Class which consisted of students who were between the ages 9-12. This gave me the opportunity to teach students who were younger than me and students who were older than me. I enjoyed this experience as well. I started seeing a lot of similarities between teaching and preaching.

Ministry is about serving

Through my work in various ministries of the church, I learned that the preacher is to do more than attend worship services and stand in the pulpit with a microphone. The preacher is to provide service to the people of the congregation. I thought that being a preacher was just about preaching. I learned that preaching and being a minister is about serving.

The word, minister, means to serve. Being a minister is about serving God, serving God's leaders, serving God's parishioners and serving God's people who are outside of the church as well. Once I extended my ministry beyond the pulpit and started serving in other areas of the church, it also opened my mind to be a minister in every area of my life.

I accepted my ministry at home and started doing my household chores and serving my family out of joy instead of obligation. I accepted my call to serve at school and began assisting my teachers and helping in various after school projects. I also accepted my role as a preacher in the community and began going out to witness with the Missionary Board. We went into the streets and passed out tracks, literature about God. We also went to the hospitals to visit the sick and the nursing homes to take care of the elderly. We served in soup kitchens and my eyes were open. I realized that I was being a good minister even though I was not preaching in the pulpit. I was a good minister because I was serving in every community that I was a part of: family, school, church and neighborhood.

Jesus Christ's example of preaching and serving

Jesus Christ taught his disciples about the importance of evangelism and community outreach. Before Jesus Christ commissioned the disciples to preach the gospel in Matthew 28:18-20, he commissioned them to serve the people in Matthew 25:34-40. He commanded his disciples to feed the hungry, provide drink to the thirsty, house the homeless, clothe the naked, visit the sick and visit those who are in prison. Jesus Christ also instructed them to serve with the proper attitude by serving people as if they were serving him. Whatever they did to the people they were doing to him. Whatever they were not doing for the people, they were not doing for him.

Jesus Christ was the greatest preacher who ever lived. Jesus Christ preached to the crowds the Gospel of the Kingdom. He taught his disciples through various parables and experiences. Nevertheless, Jesus Christ did more than preach. He was an example of service. Jesus Christ met the needs of people with whom he came in contact. He healed the sick and did good in the community (Acts 10:38). Jesus Christ met the needs of the multitudes of people who followed him. He fed the 5000 (John 6). Jesus Christ met the needs of his disciples who were closest to him. He washed their feet (John 13:14) and he cooked for them (John 21:1-14). Through Jesus Christ', example, we learn that ministry and preaching is more than lip service, it is about meeting people's needs.

Questions for Reflection

1. Outside of the pulpit, list other ways that you serve the local assembly?

2. What is your attitude towards service outside of the pulpit?

3. What areas of service do you enjoy the most?

4. What areas of service do you enjoy the least?

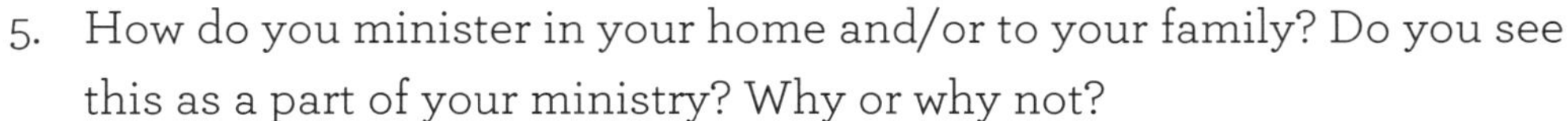

5. How do you minister in your home and/or to your family? Do you see this as a part of your ministry? Why or why not?

Questions for Reflection (continued)

6. How do you minister at work/school? Do you see this as a part of your ministry? Why or why not?

7. How do you minister in your neighborhood/the community? Do you see this as a part of your ministry? Why or why not?

8. What are some other arenas that you can preach in "outside of the four walls of the church?"

9. Outside of the examples mentioned in the text, list, describe and give biblical references of other examples of how Jesus served his disciples.

10. Outside of the examples mentioned in the text, list, describe and give biblical references of other examples of how Jesus Christ served the multitudes or groups of people outside of his disciples.

11. Outside of the examples mentioned in the text, list, describe and give biblical references of other examples of how Jesus Christ served individuals outside of his disciples.

12. List 5 biblical references that attest to the fact that Jesus Christ was a preacher.

    a.

    b.

    c.

    d.

    e.

Message #4

Sermon Title: They've Got Some Wicked Ways but They're Still My People
II Chronicles 7:12-17

Sermon Type: Textual

I. Introduction – Parents who disown their children because they don't like what they are doing or who they have become. Because they can't control them, they choose to withhold their love from them.

II. God still calls them his people – my people –even though they have wicked ways (list examples of wicked ways)

III. God stills calls them by his name – my name – even though they have wicked ways (list more examples of wicked ways)

IV. The 4 Responsibilities of God's people (humble themselves, pray, seek my face, turn from their wicked ways)

V. Conclusion – Bonus - God will always do more (eyes open, ears attentive, heart there perpetually)

Exercise

1. Change the introduction by giving three examples of how people are disowned and insert into the outline.
   A.
   B.
   C.
2. List 10 examples of wicked ways that people had in the Bible and insert them into the outline.
   1.
   2.
   3.
   4.
   5.
   6.
   7.
   8.
   9.
   10.

3. List 10 examples of wicked ways that people have in the church today and insert them into the outline.
   1.
   2.
   3.
   4.
   5.
   6.
   7.
   8.
   9.
   10.

4. Give 3 practical examples of humbling yourselves and insert them into the outline.
   a.
   b.
   c.

5. Give 3 personal examples of praying.
   a.
   b.
   c.

6. Give 3 practical examples of seeking God's face.
   a.
   b.
   c.

7. Give 3 personal examples of turning from wicked ways.
   a.
   b.
   c.

8. Give a personal example where you felt like God has given you a bonus or done more than you have expected.

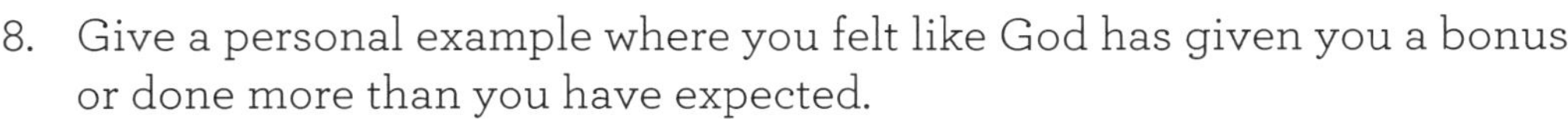

CHAPTER FIVE

THE Preacher's MOTIVES

(Age 11)

"God is going to bless you but you are not preaching for money."
Pastor Elizabeth Thompson

Go into the vineyard and work and what is right I will give you.
Matthew 20:7

Chapter Five—The Preacher's MOTIVES

I had gotten used to preaching to toilet bowls and to the atmosphere, teaching Sunday School and working around the church. After being in service to the Lord outside of the pulpit for about a year, Sister Ethel Davis, who was the President of the Usher Board, asked me to preach for the Usher's Anniversary Revival. Each year the ushers had a 5-day revival (Monday Night through Friday Night) leading up to their Anniversary Sunday. The revival had a two-fold benefit. It was a fundraiser to help the usher's reach their anniversary goal and it was a time of spiritual rejuvenation.

I told her that I would love to but I did not think Pastor Thompson had released me to preach yet. Sister Davis, who always had a sweet way about doing things, said that she had already asked Pastor Thompson and she gave me her blessings. I was so honored to be asked to preach at the Holy Name Church of Jesus. Sister Davis asked me to preach the second night of the revival, that Tuesday night. I had never preached before during the week; I had only preached on the weekends: Sunday mornings, Sunday afternoons, Friday nights and Saturday nights for Youth Services. Not only was it my first time preaching during the week, it was also my first time preaching for an occasion that was not associated with youth.

Because Tuesday night was a school night, I also had to ask my mother's permission to accept such an engagement. My mother did not normally let me go to church during the week because she did not want church to interfere with my school work. She also did not want me too tired to go to school or so tired that I was falling asleep in class. A revival service in an Apostolic Holiness Church could last for three hours. Testimony service alone could take an hour by the time that everyone sang a song, told what the Lord had done for them and danced afterwards. If the service started at 7:00 pm, then we did not get out of service until 10:00 pm. By the time we fellowshipped after service, I would not get home to 11:00 pm and I had to get up for school at 6:30 am.

Church was always my mother's leverage with me. If I did something wrong, my punishment was always that I could not go to church and I could not talk on the telephone. Church and the telephone were the only two things that meant something to me. I really did not care about room confinement or watching television or listening to music or outings. Telling me that I could not go to church was worse than beating the life out of me. My mother told me that I could accept the engagement under the following conditions:

1. I had to come straight home from school.
2. I had to take a nap after school.

3. I had to get all of my homework done before service.
4. I had to eat dinner and wash the dishes before I left for church.
5. I had to get my school clothes picked out, ironed and ready before service.
6. I had to make sure that my room and my bathroom were clean before I left for service.
7. I could not talk on the phone when I got home from church.

I gladly agreed to all of my mom's conditions. I was so happy. I invited my family, friends, classmates and neighbors to come to church that Tuesday night to hear me preach. I had never been so excited about preaching before. I felt like I had earned the right to preach in the church because I had worked so hard in the various auxiliaries of the church. I also felt worthy to preach because not only was I well integrated into the church but I had done so much community outreach outside of the church.

For the first time in my life, I felt like I was not the "cute little boy preacher." I felt like I was a real preacher. I felt like I had something of quality to say. I felt comfortable with my knowledge of the Bible and I had built a consistent prayer life. Pastor Thompson told me that this was my one chance to prove that I was indeed a preacher. She told me if I did well that I would be put in the preaching rotation. She told me if I did not do well that it would be a long time before I was given another opportunity to preach.

We were a small congregation of about 100 people. Before I was added to the preaching rotation, we had 5 preachers: Pastor Thompson, Elder Thompson (Pastor Thompson's husband), Elder Henry Davis, Minister Dorothy Taylor and Minister Katherine Robinson. We had at least 8 preaching opportunities per week; therefore, each preacher was bound to preach at least once a week. Our schedule of services was as follows:

1. Wednesday Noonday Prayer & Bible Class
2. Wednesday Night Prayer & Bible Class
3. Thursday Telecast
4. Friday Night Deliverance Service (open to the public) or Saint's Meeting Night (private for only the members of the church)
5. Sunday Morning Radio Broadcast (9:45 am – 10:30 am)*
6. Sunday School (10:30 am – 11:45am)
7. Sunday Midday Worship Service (12:00 noon – 2:30 pm)
8. Sunday Afternoon Auxiliary Service (5:00 pm – 7:30 pm)

9. Sunday Night Prayer & Bible Class (8:00 pm – 10:00 pm)

*Before the Radio Broadcast, there was Prayer on the Altar at 9:00 am. We were at church for 12-13 hours every Sunday.

In preparation for my message, I went into my closet and prayed and asked God what he wanted me to say. He gave me a vision of the ushers walking around the church and marching. I kept seeing the ushers' feet in those uniform white shoes. I researched all of the scriptures on walking and I developed the message from there. I had to keep practicing the message until I remembered what I wanted to say because Pastor Thompson did not allow us to use notes. She felt the only thing that needed to be written was the title of the message and the text. Everything else was totally based on the Spirit.

We did not have Minister's Training Class. All we received was on the job training, correction when we did something wrong and the personal nuggets that Pastor Thompson gave us one-on-one. Pastor Thompson told me, "Just open your mouth and God will fill it. If you are anointed, then God will speak through you and tell you what to say. All that you have studied and all of the scriptures that you have learned will come back to you."

For the Usher's Revival, I preached the message entitled, "Walk just like Jesus." The church was packed. It was probably the largest crowd for the entire revival. People were curious to see what this young boy could do. The message went extremely well and I got a lot of positive feedback from the audience. At the end of the service, they lifted two offerings. One was for the church and the other was for the preacher. They always announced the amount of the offerings. I don't remember how much was raised in the church offering but I remembered that my offering, the preacher's offering was $107.00. When I heard that number, I was so excited. I started thinking about all of the things that I could do with that money. I loved to dress up. I had visions of a new suit and new dress shoes.

Sister Davis asked me to stand and she had the brown envelope in her hand. I was so excited. She gave me her words of encouragement and just when she was getting ready to present me with the offering Pastor Thompson interrupted her. Pastor Thompson said, "Minister Pulley is a young preacher and we don't want him to get the wrong impression. We don't want him to think preaching is about money so if there is anyone here who has a need, Minister Pulley is going to meet that need."

She called for people who needed gas money, people who were short on a bill and people who needed lunch money to come up and receive a blessing. She made me take the money out of the brown envelope and give it to the people according to how much they needed. When we got down to $11, she said that was it that I needed to save the $11 to pay my tithes from the money that I had earned.

I was so hurt. I was so disappointed. I was praying that my hurt and disappointment did not show on my face because that would have earned me a public rebuke from Pastor Thompson. She had absolutely no problem embarrassing people in public through open rebuke. Her belief was that we all died with Jesus Christ and that we were dead to sin; therefore, a dead man does not have any feelings (Romans 6:1-10). I wanted to cry but that would have been too awkward so I just stood there and took it. I tried to grin and bear it but on the inside my heart was breaking. I went home feeling so deflated about the money but at the same time I was glad that I was put in the preaching and teaching rotation.

Although my mother was not into church the way that I was, she saw that I was hurting and tried to encourage me when I got home by telling me the following things:

1. I was too smart to just be a preacher. I should go to college and have a career as a lawyer or a writer and make big money.
2. Preaching was hobby not a full-time career. Preaching was something to do for enjoyment.
3. I did not have to depend on a preacher's offering to get the things that I wanted because I was her child and she was always going to make sure that I had what I wanted and what I needed.
4. If I believed that God called me to preach, then preaching was answering my call.

Pastor Thompson continued her practice of giving my speaker's offering away for about six months. Like working around the church and preaching to the toilet bowl, after a while I got used to not receiving money for preaching. To be honest, after the first few times, I started to enjoy giving the money away and helping the people who obviously had real financial needs.

I got to the point where I no longer expected to receive any money for preaching. To my surprise one Sunday afternoon, I was preaching for the Pastor's Aide Auxiliary and Sister Benson, the President of the Pastor's Aide Auxiliary, gave me my brown envelope. Not only was Sister Benson the President of the Pastor's Aide Auxiliary, she and her husband, Deacon Benson, owned a construction company and they were the biggest givers in the church. As I was listening to Sister Benson say, "Minister Pulley we can't pay you for the word that you preached but this is just a token of our love and appreciation for the word that you delivered," I was waiting for Pastor Thompson to get up with her normal routine of giving my offering away. Pastor Thompson did not get up and say anything about me giving it away. I was shocked. I was so happy. Again, I felt like I had earned the right to enjoy the money that I received because I did not preach for the money. I preached because God gave me a message to share with the people.

Importance of Motives

Motives are important. It's not just what we do but our reasons behind our actions are just as important. It's not just what we say but our intentions underlying our words are just as valuable as the words themselves. "God is a discerner of the thoughts and the intents of the heart (Hebrews 4:12)."

The right action with the wrong motive is still wrong. Paul, an apostle of Jesus Christ, in his first letter to the Church at Corinth talked about the importance of love being the right motivation for right actions. "And though I bestow all my goods to feed the poor, and though I give my body to be burned, and have not charity, it profits me nothing (I Corinthians 13:3)." Upon first glance of the scripture, we think that feeding the poor is charity, love in action. When we initially look at the text, we perceive that giving ones' body to be burned is also charity, love in action. Although feeding the poor is a loving action, unless the love is the motive behind feeding the poor, the act itself means nothing. Although sacrificing one's life for what he or she believes in is a noble deed, unless love is the motive underlying giving one's body to be burned, it is unprofitable.

People may see our good deeds and assume that love is our motive. God goes deeper than our deeds and our words and looks at our intentions. God goes beyond our actions and sees what's in our hearts. "Man looks on the outward appearance but God looks at the heart (I Samuel 16:7)." God is concerned not only with right actions but God is concerned about the right motives behind the right actions. With God, motives are important.

Proper Motives for Preaching

Although I did not understand it at the time, I now understand that Pastor Thompson was making sure that my motive for preaching was pure. **The first proper motive for preaching is because we love the Lord**. Jesus Christ told Peter that if you love me feed my sheep (John 21:15-18). Our love for God compels us to feed his sheep though the vehicle of preaching. Jesus did not tell Peter to feed the sheep because he loved the sheep. He told Peter to feed the sheep as a demonstration of his love for the Lord. If we preach based on people and how they treat us, then when we are hurt, disappointed and frustrated we won't want to preach. Nevertheless, if we preach because of our love for God regardless of what people do or do not do, we will still preach the Word.

Another proper motive for preaching is **because we've been called to do it**. When God calls us to preach and we answer that call with willingness and obedience, God is pleased and blesses us (Isaiah 1:19). Preaching is more than having a good testimony. Preaching is more than just having the gift of gab. Preaching is more than being a good speaker or a great orator. Preaching is a call to deliver a message from God to God's people on a consistent basis. Therefore, one of the proper motives for preaching is because God call me to preach.

Preaching because God has given you a message to share is another proper motive for preaching. Preachers are messengers. If there is no message from God, the preacher has nothing to preach. Being a preacher is like being a mail carrier. Unless someone sends some mail, the mail carrier has nothing to deliver. Being a preacher is like being a pregnant woman, unless there is a baby inside of the woman, then she doesn't have anything to deliver.

Another proper motive for preaching is **simply because you love it**. God is love and when God calls us to preach, God is calling us to love and to love what we are doing. Preaching is not designed to be a chore but a joy. Preaching is to be enjoyed. When we love what we are doing, it's not work; it's fun.

Improper Motives for Preaching

Just as there are proper motives for preaching, there are several improper motives for preaching. People are motivated to do what they do for different reasons; therefore, it is important that we examine our motives and intentions to be sure that they are pure. **Some of the improper motives for preaching are preaching for payment, for prestige or for a platform.**

There are several scriptures that speak about being a blessing to the man or woman of God who preaches the gospel. Jesus Christ said, "The laborer is worthy of his hire (Luke 10:7)." Paul, an apostle built on the foundation Jesus Christ laid, and wrote about the preacher giving spiritual things to the congregation and the congregation giving natural things to the preacher (I Corinthians 9:11). As professionals who are called by God and properly trained to preach, we are to be compensated for the work of ministry (Ephesians 4:11-13).

Although I appreciate whatever congregations give me for preaching, I learned early on in my ministry that the people did not have enough money to pay me for what I did. The honorariums that we receive are not equivalent to the time, energy and experiences that are involved in receiving and delivering a message. There is a part that the congregation gives us for preaching and teaching and then there is an additional portion that God rewards us with that goes above and beyond our expectations (Ephesians 3:20).

Due to Pastor Thompson's influence, I never preach for money. Money is never my motivation for preaching. I don't preach because I love money. Preachers who are motivated by money are susceptible to moral dilemmas (sex, drugs, crime). "The love of money is the root of all evil (I Timothy 6:10)." I preach because I love God. Because we love God, we are encouraged to "feed the flock of God which is among you, taking the oversight thereof, not by constraint, but willingly; not for filthy lucre, but of a ready mind (I Peter 5:2)."

Another improper motive for preaching is preaching for prestige. Some people see becoming a preacher as an opportunity to be revered. Some people are not able to be successful in any other arena so they use the church and the pulpit as an opportunity to gain fame and fortune. These preachers are motivated by pride and ego. They have a deep need for people to look up to them and tell them how great they are. Most of the time when you are preaching, you are in a position where you are standing up and others are sitting down; therefore, they have to look up at you.

For unhealthy preachers, preaching is an attempt to fill the emptiness that they feel inside. Because they suffer from low self-esteem, lack of self-worth and poor self-image, these preachers are often vulnerable to inappropriate relationships with their parishioners. Preaching is not about boosting the ego but delivering the message that God has given us.

Another improper motive for preaching is using the pulpit as a platform to express our personal opinions, ideologies and politics. Preaching is about delivering God's message to God's people, not asserting our agendas to get a point across. The pulpit is not a place to throw slurs or to throw stones at people. If you have something that you need to say to someone, pull the person aside and say it. Abstain from using the pulpit or the preaching moment as an opportunity to get things off your chest that you always wanted to say. Consider your audience and make sure that you are not just talking to hear yourself talk but you are delivering God's message to God's people.

Questions for Reflection

1. What do you think about Pastor Thompson's practice of giving away the young preacher's offerings for a period of time? Do you agree or disagree with this practice? Explain why.

2. What do you think about the advice that the young preacher's mother gave him regarding honorariums? Of time? Do you agree or disagree with this advice? Explain why.

Questions for Reflection (continued)

3. Do you have a set honorarium when you accept preaching engagements? Why or why not?

4. Why are motives and intentions important?

5. List 3 proper motives for preaching. They can be the ones listed in the reading, additional motives or a combination of both.

6. Which proper motive resonates with you most? Why?

7. Which proper motive resonates with you least? Why?

8. List 3 improper motives for preaching. They can be the ones listed in the reading, additional motives or a combination of both.

9. Which improper motive resonates with you most? Why?

10. Which improper motive resonates with you least? Why?

Message #5

Sermon Title: Walk Just Like Jesus - I John 2:1-6

Sermon Type: Topical

I. Introduction

A. Ushers do a lot of walking.

B. Jesus was an usher. He walked on water. He walked through the towns ushering people into a closer relationship with God.

II. John was a preacher of Christ who walked like Jesus and in his epistles. He taught believers how to walk, how to live.

A. Walk in the Light (I John 1:5-7)

B. Knowledge and awareness of God's presence in your life.

C. Let the light bulb come on for you

III. Walk in Love (II John 1:6)

A. Love God.

B. Love Yourself.

C. Love Everyone Else

IV. Walk in Truth (III John 1:4).

A. Be honest with God

B. Be honest with yourself

C. Be honest with others

V. Conclusion – You may not be a member of the Usher Board but you need to check your walk, your life.

Exercise

1. Give 3 scriptural references of Jesus walking.

2. Research and list 5 additional facts about the writer of I, II and III John.

3. The points of the message are in sequential order. What do you think about the way the points of the message are ordered (light, love and truth)?

4. List points in order of importance. List them in ascending order (least important to most important) and give your rationale for the order. List the points in descending order (most important to least important) and give your rationale for the order.

5. The light bulb is an image that people can relate to in order to help them connect with walking in the light. What image can you use to help people relate to walking in love?

6. What image can you use to help people relate to walking in truth?

7. The points walking in love and walking in truth are developed in the same manner (God, self and others). Choose another way to develop either walking in love or walking in truth. List the new sub points that you created. Explain why you chose to change love or truth.

8. Besides walking, what is another important aspect of ushering that can be developed into a message?

9. Using the example above, create a message outline developing this aspect of ushering. Be sure it has a title, a text, an introduction, 3 points and a conclusion.

Exercise Workspace

CHAPTER SIX

THE Preacher's PREPARATION

(Age 12)

"You should be able to preach at the drop of a dime."
Pastor Elizabeth Thompson

Preach the Word and be instant in season and out of season.
I Timothy 4:2

Chapter Six—The Preacher's PREPARATION

I was so excited to be in the preaching rotation at the Holy Name Church of Jesus. I felt like I could finally breathe again because I was preaching again. I felt like myself again because I was back to doing what God had called me to do, preach. Along with the excitement about preaching, I also felt anxiety and frustration around preaching. Although I knew that I was preaching at least bi-weekly and sometimes weekly, the anxiety came from the fact that we never knew exactly when we were going to preach. It was also frustrating because I could not invite family and friends to hear me preach because I didn't know when I was preaching.

Pastor Thompson governed the preaching schedule personally and you dare not ask her when you were going to preach. She said, "The Lord always tells me who has the Word that the church needs to hear." I believed the Lord did tell her who was supposed to preach. I just didn't understand why he always told her at the last minute.

As a young preacher, preaching had a hierarchy. Delivering the Sunday Midday message was more important to me than a Friday Night or Sunday afternoon. There were more people in church during the Sunday Midday Worship experience. I also felt that preaching on the radio held more weight than Sunday Midday because there was a larger listening audience. I deemed preaching on television higher than preaching on the radio because the patronage was broader and they could see you. Pastor Thompson; however, did not share the same idea of a preaching hierarchy as I did. She felt that if you could preach, then you could preach anytime, anywhere and to anybody.

The first time I preached on radio, I did not know that I was preaching until the radio announcer, Elder Dorothy Taylor said, "After this selection by the choir, the next voice you will hear will be that of Minister Doral R. Pulley." I was not prepared. I only had the time while the choir was singing to prepare a message that would be delivered to a radio audience. I prayed in my heart, "Lord, let the choir sing a long song and let a shout break out so that I can have more time to get the message together." The Lord answered the first part of my prayer so I had about seven minutes to pull it together. I felt like I was being thrown into the water and forced to swim. I could hear the words of Pastor Thompson in my mind saying, "You better preach!"

By God's grace, the message went over well. I preached the message, "DWI, Deal With It!" But I learned a powerful lesson, **always be prepared**. I promised God, Pastor Thompson and myself that I would never be caught in that position again. I will always be prepared to preach.

After the radio broadcast, Pastor Thompson pulled in her office and told me how proud she was of me. She told me "if you are a true preacher, then you have to be able to preach at the drop of a dime. I should be able to call you at 2:00 in the morning and say Preach, Pulley and you should be able to preach." For Pastor Thompson, it was simple, "That's what preachers do, preach." Singers sing. Teachers teach. Painters paint. Writers write. Cooks cook. Preachers preach.

Preparation through prayer

Prayer is an important spiritual discipline for every believer, especially preachers. The kings, the prophets and the priests of the Old Testament prayed to God. One example is King David in 2 Samuel 7:27, he prayed, "For thou, O Lord of hosts, God of Israel, hast revealed to thy servant, saying, I will build thee an house: therefore hath thy servant found in his heart to pray this prayer unto thee..."

Prayer was an important topic in the ministry of Jesus Christ and the apostles. During the Sermon on the Mountain recorded in Matthew 6:5-6, Jesus Christ taught his disciples "when you pray, enter into thy closet, and when thou hast shut thy door, pray to thy Father which is in secret; and thy Father which sees in secret shall reward thee openly." He also gave his disciples a particular pattern to use for prayer in Matthew 6:9-14 "After this manner therefore pray: Our Father which art in heaven, Hallowed be thy name..." In addition to teaching his disciples about prayer and giving them a pattern for prayer, Jesus Christ taught parables about the importance of prayer, " Luke 18:1 states, "And he spoke a parable unto them to this end, that men ought always to pray, and not to faint."

In a general epistle, James, an apostle of Jesus Christ, wrote, "Pray one for another, that ye may be healed. The effectual fervent prayer of a righteous man avails much (James 5:7)." It is imperative for our spiritual growth and development that we establish a regular routine which includes times of personal and corporate prayer. Some people pray best in the morning at the start of the day. Others have the most effective prayer at night at the close of the day before they go to bed. It does not matter when you prayer as long as you have a time set aside to meet God in prayer.

Pastor Thompson used to say all the time "If preachers aren't praying then I don't know what they are preaching." Pastor Thompson was a woman of prayer. We had prayer at the church at least 30 minutes prior to each service and you better pray. When Pastor Thompson came out of her office, she would walk around the church praying in a loud deep voice. She would go up and down the aisles and through every pew making sure that people were praying. After her prayer walk, she would get on the microphone and pray until heaven came down and glory filled the temple.

I learned from Pastor Thompson that prayer was essential to the life of a preacher. Before coming to Holy Name Church of Jesus, I did not know much about prayer. Although I was a young preacher, nobody taught me how to pray for any length of time. I knew how to say a minute prayer when I woke up in the morning thanking God for another day. I knew how to say a 30 second grace over my food. I knew how to say the Lord's Prayer and "Now a lay me down to sleep" before I went to bed. I also knew how to pray for about 90 seconds if I was called to do an invocation in a service. I knew how to pray with people at the altar and lead them to Christ which normally took a minute or two.

Jesus Christ asked his disciples, why they "could not watch and pray with him for one hour (Matthew 26:36-46)?" Before meeting Pastor Thompson, the idea of praying an hour was foreign to me. I could not even pray 30 minutes or 15 minutes. I recommend that preachers spend at least an hour in prayer every day. Prayer equips the preacher with right perspective, right hearing and the right message.

In prayer, God shows us ourselves. I'm leery of people who pray and God tells them about everybody but themselves. I am cautious of people who have a word for everyone else but God did not tell them about themselves. When I pray, God first shows me, myself. Unless I can see myself clearly, I can't properly see others. In the Sermon on the Mount, Jesus Christ, taught his disciples that they must first get the beam out of their own eyes before they were able to see the mote in the eye of their brother or sister (Matthew 7:3-5).

When Isaiah, the prophet, had the heavenly vision of cherubims and seraphims, the first person that Isaiah saw was himself. "Woe is me! For I am undone; because I am a man of unclean lips (Isaiah 6:5a)." The scriptures do not tell us what made Isaiah's lips unclean. We don't know if it was profanity, vulgarity, lying, gossiping or being double-tongued. We just know that he had a problem with his mouth. Often the area in which we have the most challenge is the area of our lives that God wants to manifest his glory.

After Isaiah saw himself, he could then clearly see the people. Isaiah saw that he and the people had some things in common. "I dwell among a people of unclean lips (Isaiah 6:5b)." He recognized that both he and the people had unclean lips. In order to be an effective preacher, we have to be able to relate to people and identify with what they are experiencing. We have to be able to see ourselves in the people and see the people in us. The Law of Demonstration reminds us that "like begets like." We can only bring forth fruit after our own kind (Genesis 1:11-12). What we see in others is really what we see in ourselves.

Through prayer not only does God show us our impurities, **God cleanses us of our impurities**. After Isaiah prayed and saw that he was not any different from the people, God cleaned him up. "Then flew one of the seraphims unto me, having a live coal in his hand, which he had taken with the tongs from off the altar: And he laid it upon my mouth, and said, Lo, this hath touched thy lips; and thine iniquity is taken away, and thy sin purged

(Isaiah 6:6-7)."

We can't preach to others effectively if we are not clean ourselves. We have to allow God to cleanse us so that the Word of God can flow through a pure vessel. No matter how good the meal is nobody wants to eat it off of a dirty plate. No matter how tasty the beverage is nobody wants to drink it out of a dirty glass.

We must stay in the presence of God through prayer long enough so that God can cleanse us of our unrighteousness. It took time for the seraphim to fly to the altar. It took time for the seraphim to get the tongs off of the altar. It took time for the seraphim to get the coal with the tongs. It took time for the seraphim to lay the hot coal on Isaiah's mouth long enough to cleanse his lips.

Notice that the coal did not destroy Isaiah's mouth, it only cleansed it. In prayer, when God shows us ourselves, it is not to condemn us or to make us feel ashamed of ourselves or guilty about our thoughts, words or behaviors. All God desires to do is cleanse us so that we are available to minister to his people. After Isaiah was clean, God asked, "whom shall I send and who will go for us (Isaiah 6:8a)?" After Isaiah was purified through the hot coal, Isaiah responded, "here am I send me (Isaiah 6:8b)." **Prayer empowered Isaiah to say, "Yes" to God.**

After Isaiah was cleansed and he made himself available to God, **in prayer God gave him the message to give to the people.** "And he said, Go, and tell this people, Hear ye indeed, but understand not; and see ye indeed, but perceive not (Isaiah 6:9)." Isaiah was given a specific word for a specific people for a specific time. Through prayer, God gives us a Rhema word to give to his people.

In addition to the message, **through prayer God made clear to Isaiah what his assignment was.** "Make the heart of this people fat, and make their ears heavy, and shut their eyes (Isaiah 6:10)." Through prayer, we are not only clear about the word to preach but we gain insight on our assignment and the intention of the Word that we are given to preach. God lets us know what results should take place through the message: miracles, signs, wonders, healing, deliverance, financial breakthrough, order, repentance, etc.

Prayer is a two communication between you and God. Therefore, not only did God talk to Isaiah but Isaiah talked to God. **Through prayer, Isaiah was also able to ask questions about the message and the assignment that God had given him.** "Then said I, Lord, how long? And he answered, until the cities be wasted without inhabitant, and the houses without man, and the land be utterly desolate." Through prayer, we can obtain the same cleansing and clarity that Isaiah received.

In prayer, God gives you the message and tells you what to say to the people. How can you know what the people need if you are not praying? How will you know what message is for what congregation if you are not praying? Prayer is the major distinguishing factor between a message and a sermon.

Under the leadership of Pastor Thompson, not only were we always praying but regularly we fasted from various food and beverages. Most of the fasts were absolute fasts with no food and no water for three days, five days or even seven days. Through prayer and consecration, I became familiar with God's voice and I was able to distinguish it from my own voice and the voice of others. "My sheep know my voice and a stranger they will not follow (John 10:27)." Because I was so used to hearing God's voice, in prayer, when I was not in prayer I could also hear clearly God's voice speaking to me throughout my day during my normal activities.

Preparation through Purity

I learned that preparation for preaching is more than just studying the Word of God and staying in prayer but it was also about purity. In order for us to be effective preachers, we have to keep our hearts pure. When our hearts are pure, we see God in every person, in every place and in everything (Matthew 5:8). In order for us to be effective preachers, we have to keep our spirits free. David knew the importance of having a free spirit. David prayed, "...Uphold me with thy free spirit (Psalms 51:12)." It's challenging to preach over mess in our own lives. God desires us to be clean vessels.

One way to keep our hearts pure and our spirits free from guilt, shame and condemnation is by making sure that we don't have any unconfessed sin in my lives. There are various definitions for sin:

1. The transgression of God's laws and principles – I John 3:4
2. Missing the mark – Psalms 37:37
3. Doing what God told us not to do – Genesis 2:16-17
4. Omitting to do what God told us to do – James 4:17
5. Self-Inflicted Non-Sense - James 1:13-15

We all make poor choices. We think, say and do things that are not in accordance with God's perfect, will and plan for our lives. When we are wrong, we must admit it, confess it and forsake it. "Confess your faults one to another (James 5:16)." It is important to expose darkness to the light. The longer we hide our sins, the deeper we go into them. "He that covers his sins shall not prosper: but whoso confesses and forsakes them shall have mercy (Proverbs 28:13)."

Another way to keep our hearts pure and spirits free from anger, bitterness and unforgiveness is to resolve conflicts as quickly as possible. "Let not the sun go down on your wrath (Ephesians 4:26)." It is important to resolve any conflicts within a 24-hour period of time. Whether we do it with the person or within our own consciousness, we must let it go.

Jesus Christ taught his disciples various methods to deal with conflict. In Matthew 18:15-18, Jesus Christ addressed how to deal with a situation when someone has done us wrong. He gave them steps to follow so that this type of conflict can be resolved:

1. Go to the person alone
2. Take a neutral non-bias third party
3. Go to the church
4. Put the person out of the church

In Matthew 5:23-24, Jesus Christ also taught his disciples how to address the case if a person has an issue with them:

1. Before you operate in your gift, do an assessment.
2. If you are clear, minister in your gift.

If you remember that someone has something against you,

1. Leave your (unpresented) gift at the altar
2. Be reconciled with your brother or sister
3. Bring your gift (presented) to the altar

If we follow this method, then we will have harmonious relationships and peaceful interactions.

Preparation through Possibilities

In addition to preparing through prayer and preparing through purity, we must also be prepared for endless preaching possibilities. We must be open for God to speak to us and give us messages through various resources: radio, television shows, commercials, movies, songs, plays, conversations, experiences, dreams, visions, etc. We must also be open to try things that we have never tried before in our preaching (a different type of message, a different way of delivering it, etc.). We must be open to various outcomes of the message. We never know how God is going to manifest his presence through us or in the midst of the congregation, so we must be prepared for endless possibilities.

Questions for Reflection

1. What lesson did the young preacher learn from preaching on the radio?

2. Do you agree with the young preacher's hierarchy of preaching? Why or why not?

3. Do you agree with Pastor Thompson's method of scheduling preachers? Why or why not?

4. How often do you preach? Why?

5. How much notice are you normally given to prepare for a message? Why?

6. Do you do better with long preaching notices or short preaching notices? Why?

7. List 5 ways that a person can receive a message.

    a.

    b.

    c.

    d.

    e.

Questions for Reflection (continued)

7. Which method of reception resonates with you most? Which method of reception resonates with you least?

8. List 2 definitions for sin.
   a.
   b.

9. Which type of sin do you commit most often? Why?

10. What is the major difference between a sermon and a message?

11. List 5 ways that prayer prepares a preacher to give a message.
    a.
    b.
    c.
    d.
    e.

12. Describe your current prayer life (when, where, how often, how long).

13. How can you improve your prayer life?

14. List 2 ways that the preacher can keep his heart pure and his spirit free.

Questions for Reflection (continued)

15. What methods do you employ to keep your heart pure and your spirit free?

16. Outline the stages that Isaiah experienced in preparation for God's message and assignment for him.

17. Give another example of a biblical figure who endured great preparation to be God's messenger. Give the scriptural references.

Message #6

Sermon Title: DWI - Deal With It!
Sermon Type: Biographical

I. Introduction
   A. Attention – DWI – Driving While Intoxicated and its impact on you and others. But that's not what I'm talking about.
   B. In order to become the person that God desires us to become, we have to deal with a whole lot of stuff. Many are the afflictions of the righteous but God delivers them out of them all.

II. Dealing with the Pit – sold into slavery by his brothers just because he had a dream. Dealing with family issues (Genesis 37:24-27)

III. Dealing with the Prison – lied on by Potiphar's wife. Dealing with persecution outside of family (Genesis 39:9-20)

IV. Dealing with the Palace – interpreting Pharaoh's dream. Not being afraid of Pharaoh to say what thus says the Lord. Allowing your gift to make room for you at the proper time (Genesis 41:14-45)

V. Conclusion – The process is developing a product of quality, Joseph, a person who can handle being second in command to Pharaoh with both the famine and the feast (Genesis 41:53-57).

Exercise

1. **Give** a personal experience of dealing with or being effected by a DWI.
2. **Read** Genesis 37:24-27 and describe the type of family issues Joseph faced.
3. **Give** a personal experience of a family issue that you have encountered.
4. **List** several current issues that families face today.
5. **Why** did Potiphar's wife lie on Joseph?
6. **Give** a personal example where you lied on somebody.
7. **Give** a personal example where somebody lied on you.
8. **Besides** imprisonment, what other impacts can lies have on people's lives?
9. List various ways that a person's gift can make room for him or her.
10. How often do you dream?
11. How do you interpret your dreams?
12. List all of the "P" words in the message.
13. **Choose** another male biblical character and outline a message using the details of his life story.
14. **Choose** a female biblical character and outline a message using the details of her life story.

Exercise Workspace

CHAPTER SEVEN

THE EVALUATION of a Preacher

(Age 13)

"You are good but you can always get better."
Pastor Elizabeth Thompson

Examine yourselves...prove your own selves.
II Corinthians 13:5

CHAPTER SEVEN—The EVALUATION of a Preacher

I was the Director of the Youth Choir at church. I made it a habit to record the choir so that we could play the tape back in rehearsal and actually hear how we sounded. Hearing how we sounded empowered us to celebrate the good parts and improve on the "not so good parts." I tried to employ the same strategy for preaching.

Whenever I preached, someone normally recorded the message on their personal tape recorder. However, the quality of the recording was not that great. I could hardly hear myself over the noise of the audience and the person recording the message. The tape from the first time that I preached on radio and the video from the first time that I preached on television provided me with the quality recording to really evaluate my preaching.

The first thing that I noticed while listening and watching myself was my high squeaky voice. These recordings were done during puberty right while my voice was in the midst of changing. I did not like the sound of my voice especially how it would go up and down mid-sentence. Once I got passed the sound of my voice, I was able to evaluate myself and use what I saw and what I heard to improve my preaching.

Pastor Thompson gave words of encouragement every now and then, but there was no formal evaluation process for preachers. The preachers of my local assembly did not really talk about how to improve our preaching. We did not see preaching as an art form; we saw it as a spiritual activity. As long as we did not misquote the scriptures, go against the doctrine/dogma of the church or mix up the details of the text, people just talked about how good the message was especially if people shouted at the end of the message.

Overtime, I developed the Pulley Preaching Pointers and the Message Evaluation Form as a way to help preachers do a better job preaching. The two instruments work together. They are tools to get preachers to at least talk about preaching and how to help each other improve.

Need for Evaluation

"Practice makes perfect" is a familiar quote that people often use to encourage people to work on their craft. I'm not sure that practice makes perfect because I did not think that perfection can be obtained in this physical existence. Paul, an apostle of Jesus Christ, said "not as though I have already attained or were already perfect...but I press toward the mark for the prize of the high calling of God in Christ Jesus (Philippians 3:13-16)."

The goal of preaching is not perfection but improvement over time. The more we do something, the better we are at what we are doing. It is proper ministerial etiquette to wait to be asked to preach in our home churches or at guest churches. Therefore, it is important for preachers to seek other opportunities to preach whenever they can. Preaching is not limited to being behind the pulpit in the local assembly. Preaching can be done on the streets, in prisons, nursing homes and rehabilitation centers. The more we preach, the more there is an opportunity for evaluation. There are four major types of evaluation: self-evaluation, mentor evaluation, peer evaluation and audience evaluation. Regardless of the type of evaluation, preachers must always be ready and willing to receive constructive criticism about the message. Sometimes evaluations will be given in the spirit of love and support. Sometimes evaluations may seem like a dagger right through the heart. Regardless of who gives the feedback and how they present it, accept it because it can only make you a better preacher.

Self-Evaluation

The most important evaluation is self-evaluation. The scriptures speak of self-examination (I Corinthians 11:27-31, II Corinthians 13:5). Self-evaluation is paramount because only the preacher knows what God has commanded him or her to say and/or do. Only you know if you said what God told you to say in the very best way that you are able to say it. Only you know if you did what God told you to do in the very best way that you are able do it.

Some important questions to ask yourself that will stimulate the self-evaluation process are:

1. How did I do (overall)?
2. Did I say what God told me to say to the best of my ability? Why or why not?
3. Did I do what God told me to do to the best of my ability? Why or why not?
4. What did I like about the message?
5. What did not I like about the message?
6. How can I make it better?
7. Given an opportunity to do it over, what will I do differently next time?
8. How is the way that I envisioned the message similar to the way that the message actually took place?
9. How is the way that I envisioned the message different from the way that the message actually took place?
10. Did the message feed me? Why or why not?

Mentor Evaluation

Every preacher needs a mentor. A mentor is someone who has been where you are and who is in the place that you aspire to be. A preacher can help another preacher get better at preaching. I admired Pastor Thompson not only as a pastor but as a preacher. I was always amazed at the revelation knowledge that she could pull from a text. She preached with great conviction and her delivery compelled people to change. Whenever she was willing to share something with me about preaching, I was always willing to listen. She was the expert and I was the novice. She was a founding pastor of two congregations and was well established on radio and television.

Paul, an apostle of Jesus Christ, told Timothy, his son in the gospel, "Consider what I say and the Lord will give you understanding in all things (II Timothy 2:7)." We may not always like what our mentor says, but we are to give their words great weight. We may not understand everything that our mentor does, but we are to give their actions great consideration.

The writer of Hebrews admonished the church about the importance of spiritual mentors. "Remember them which have the rule over you, who have spoken unto you the word of God: whose faith follow, considering the end of their conversation (Hebrews 13:7)." Preachers have a lot of power and authority; therefore, it is essential that preachers are under the authority of a spiritual leader, someone who has authority over them. It is also important that preachers be fed and that someone is speaking the word of God in and over their lives. Mentors are also examples of faith. They encourage us that if God did it for them then God can do it for me. Finally, mentors stimulate growth and development in the preacher through their conversations, critiques and lifestyles.

Peer Evaluation

In addition to self-evaluation and mentor evaluation, preachers can benefit from the evaluation of peers in ministry. Peers are those who are in the same ministry classes that you are in or those who share your same level of ministry. Peer review has a different slant than a mentor. Peers are listening to the message and looking at you from an equal status. They catch things that mentors might miss. As peers, we give each other a different type of support and critique.

Colleagues in ministry are necessary. They understand exactly where we are and what we are experiencing. Peers can also be a great source to bounce message ideas off of and get their feedback. Sometimes, what they say may hurt our feelings because they may not have the same tact as a mentor but "faithful are the wounds of a friend (Proverbs 27:6)." We must be open to receive evaluation from our peers and see the relationship as "iron sharpens iron (Proverbs 27:17)."

Audience Feedback

It is also beneficial to the preacher to get audience feedback and evaluation. Sometimes, people will shake your hand after service and tell you exactly how they were blessed by the message. Pay close attention to what they say. Other times people will just greet you and say that the message was good. See this as an opportunity to get their feedback. Ask them what it was about the message that resonated with them. Don't be afraid to engage them in dialogue about the message; it is a learning opportunity.

Listening with a different ear

Being trained how to preach does not exempt you from receiving God's messages to you from other preachers. Sometimes, we can get so caught up in evaluating other preachers that we forget that we too are disciples of Jesus Christ who need the Word of God for our own holistic growth and development. We can't get so caught up in critiquing other preachers that we miss God's word for our own lives. It is essential that we make a clear distinction between those times when we are listening with the ear of evaluation and when we are just members of the congregation looking to receive a word from the Lord. There is a time and a season for every purpose under heaven (Ecclesiastes 3:1).

Questions for Reflection

1. Do you evaluate yourself after you preach? Why or why not?
2. Which self-evaluation question resonated with you most? Why?
3. Which self-evaluation question resonated with you least? Why?
4. Who is your preaching mentor?
5. How did he or she become your mentor?
6. Describe the quality of evaluation that you receive from your mentor.
7. List and describe 3 of your colleagues in ministry.
8. Describe the quality of critique that you receive from them.
9. Describe a time when you received feedback from the audience after service. How did you respond to that feedback?
10. What is the difference between audience feedback during the message and audience feedback after the message?
11. What is the difference between constructive and destructive criticism?
12. Compare and contrast the two different ears when listening to a message.

Message #7

Sermon Title: Everything You Need is in the Garden! Genesis 2:7-25

Sermon Type: Textual

I. Introduction – The garden represents the presence of God. Everything that we need to find fulfillment in life is in the garden.

II. There was eternal life in the garden. There was no death. They had to leave the garden to die.

III. There was perfect health in the garden. There was no sickness, pain or disease in the garden.

IV. There was perfect provision in the garden. There was no lack or poverty in the garden. They could eat of all the trees in the garden and be full.

V. There were leadership opportunities in the garden. They ruled over the fish of the sea, the birds of the air and the animals that walked the earth.

VI. There was a career in the garden. Taking care of the garden, dressing and keeping it.

VII. There was love and companionship in the garden. God gave Eve to Adam in the garden.

VIII. Conclusion – There are presents in his presence. In the presence of God is the fullness of joy and at his right hand there are pleasures forevermore.

Exercise

1. List scriptural references that speak of the presence of God.
2. Give a scriptural reference for each point of the message (I – VIII).
3. If there was a point that you could add to the message, what would it be? Why?
4. If there was a point that you could delete from the message, what would it be? Why?
5. What do you think about the play on words strategy of "presents and presence"?
6. Give 3 other examples of the play on word strategy.
7. Create an introduction that deals with gardens and how they are used today.
8. Give a personal example for 3 of the points of the message.
9. What can you do or say to paint the picture of the Garden of Eden to make the audience feel that they are right there with Adam and Eve.

Exercise Workspace

Exercise Workspace

CHAPTER EIGHT

THE Preacher's EXPECTATION

(Age 14)

"When you preach, expect something to happen."
Pastor Elizabeth Thompson

For there shall be a performance of those things which were told her from the Lord.
Luke 1:45

CHAPTER EIGHT—The Preacher's EXPECTATION

I was always amazed by the ministry of Pastor Elizabeth Thompson. It was not just that her preaching was good, but because something always happened every time she preached. I just never knew what was going to happen.

After about a year of going to Holy Name Church of Jesus, my mother starting going to church with me. My mother wanted to know what type of church captivated her son so that he was interested in going every time the doors were opened. My mother was paralyzed from the fire but she came to church with assistance and used the wheelchair ramp. One Friday night we were in church and Pastor Thompson preached. After preaching the message, she made an altar call and my mother raised her hand and said that she wanted to be saved. Salvation in Holy Name meant getting baptized, fully immersed in water, in the name of the Lord Jesus Christ and being filled with the Holy Ghost with the manifestation of speaking in other tongues.

My mother started crying as she told Pastor Thompson that she wanted to be saved but she was afraid. She was afraid of getting baptized because she was a large woman and thought she might drown. She did not think that the brothers in the church would be able to dip her in the water and lift her out of the pool. Pastor Thompson told my mother that she did not have to worry about drowning. Pastor Thompson encouraged my mother when she said, "By faith, you walk in the pool and walk out of the pool." My mother believed God and was healed from her paralysis right before my very eyes. My mother walked in and out of the baptismal pool and came out of the water speaking in other tongues. The church danced and shouted for hours because a miracle had taken place. Overtime my mother went from the wheelchair, to the walker, to the cane and finally she was able to walk without any assistance. As a result of the preached Word and expectancy something happened.

I was so happy to see my mother walk again. I thanked Pastor Thompson over and over again for being a vessel of God. Pastor Thompson told me, "The same miracles can take place through your ministry. When you preach, you just have to expect something to happen."

At 14, I preached my first 3-day Revival in Chase City, Virginia at Holy Name Church of Jesus #2. Pastor Thompson had established her second church in her husband's, Elder Hural Thompson's, hometown. I was so excited about the opportunity to do a 3-day Revival. Elder Thompson and Pastor Thompson drove me to Chase City. During the ride, Pastor Thompson gave me some pointers about doing a revival:

1. Choose a topic or a text that is broad enough to cover three days.
2. Break the topic or text down into three parts.
3. Pull different perspectives and principles from the same text to keep it interesting.
4. Don't spill into the next night's message.
5. At the end of each message give the people a hook.
6. The hook that will keep them hungry wanting more.
7. The hook will make them come back the next night.
8. The hook will inspire them to invite someone else to come with them.
9. Be prepared to do prayer lines each night for salvation, healing and deliverance.
10. Greet the people after service and make personal contact with them.
11. Fast and pray during the day so that you will be spiritually prepared to minister each night.
12. Review the previous night's message for those who were there as reinforcement.
13. Summarize the previous night's message to catch people up who were not there the night before.
14. Let the people set a goal for what they desire to see done by the end of the revival. Create a sense of expectancy.
    a. Healing
    b. Salvation
    c. Deliverance

When we arrived in the country town of Chase City, there was so much excitement. There was such a sense of expectancy in the air. Members of the church were there to greet us and welcome us into their homes. We did not stay in hotels; we stayed with the saints. During the day, we did evangelistic work. We went to the radio station to promote the revival and passed out fliers in the major traffic areas. We went from house to house inviting the people to come see the young preacher. We went from door to door witnessing and inviting people to revival.

We visited an elderly lady who was blind. She asked us to pray for her. I asked what she desired prayer for and she said that she desired to see. Therefore, I laid hands on her eyes and prayed for God to restore her sight. After the prayer, she screamed, "I can see." I was so afraid and shocked that I abruptly left the house and ran back to the car. Although I had prayed for her sight, I really wasn't expecting anything to happen, especially not immediately. As I sat in the car waiting for the other church members who were witnessing, Pastor Thompson's word came back to me, "You have to expect something to happen after you minister to people." I was also reminded of the scriptures when the saints were praying for Peter to be released from prison. When Peter came to the door where they were praying no one would open it because they were not expecting their prayers to be answered so soon (Acts 12:5-17). Whenever we pray, preach, sing or minister in any way, we must expect the manifestation of God's presence in extraordinary ways.

The lady whose sight was restored came to church that night and brought other people with her. I was so nervous. She kept pointing at me saying, "That's the boy that healed me." I did not like the pressure of people coming to me expecting a miracle. Nevertheless, I found comfort in the fact that I was not the healer or the miracle worker. I was just a vessel through which the Spirit flowed. It was the combination of her faith and the power of God that healed her (Mark 5:34, II Corinthians 5:7, II Timothy 2:20-21).

When Jesus Christ Preached Something Happened

The Gospel of Jesus Christ is the birth, life, death, burial, resurrection, ascension and Second Coming of Jesus Christ (Mark 1:1, Romans 1:16, I Corinthians 15:11-22). Jesus Christ did not preach the Gospel of Jesus Christ. He was the Gospel of Jesus Christ. His life and ministry is what we know today as the Gospel of Jesus Christ. The Gospel of Jesus Christ is what brings people to salvation.

Jesus Christ preached the Gospel of the Kingdom. The Kingdom of God is a system a form of government, a way of being, seeing, thinking, speaking and behaving in which God is the center. The Kingdom of God is when God's will in heaven is done on the earth. "Thy Kingdom come, thy will be done on earth as it is in heaven (Matthew 6:10)." The Kingdom is the king's domain; it is the place where the king rules and reigns. "Behold, the Kingdom of God is within you (Luke 17:21)." The Kingdom of God is not anything physical or temporal and has no geographical location. "The Kingdom of God is not meat or drink but righteousness, peace and joy in the Holy Ghost (Romans 14:17)." The Gospel of the Kingdom of God teaches people how to live out their salvation.

Jesus Christ taught about the Kingdom of God. Most of Jesus Christ's parables begin with the Kingdom of God is like ... or the Kingdom of Heaven is like...Jesus Christ used physical things that people could relate to teach them Kingdom Principles. Jesus Christ used natural things that people could identify with to illustrate what the Kingdom was all about. In Matthew 13 alone, there are 7 parables that Jesus Christ used to exemplify the Kingdom of God.

"And Jesus went about all Galilee, teaching in their synagogues, and preaching the gospel of the kingdom, and healing all manner of sickness and all manner of disease among the people (Matthew 4:23)." Whenever and wherever Jesus Christ preached and taught the Gospel of the Kingdom, something happened (Matthew 9:35). People's lives were no longer the same. Whoever received the Gospel of the Kingdom was changed forever.

John the Baptist, who was the forerunner of Jesus Christ, reached a point in his life where he questioned the ministry of Jesus Christ that he once endorsed. John the Baptist was unsure as to whether or not Jesus Christ was actually the one whom they had been waiting for; therefore, he sent his disciples to gather information. They received more than they expected. "Jesus answered and said unto them, Go and show John again those things which ye do hear and see: the blind receive their sight, and the lame walk, the lepers are cleansed, and the deaf hear, the dead are raised up, and the poor have the gospel preached to them (Matthew 11:4-5)."

Jesus Christ Taught His Apostles to Expect Something

The disciples of Jesus Christ were called to continue the ministry of Jesus Christ. Therefore, they needed signs, wonders and miracles following their ministries as well. When Jesus Christ first commissioned them into ministry, he taught them to expect something. "He gave them power against unclean spirits, to cast them out, and to heal all manner of sickness and all manner of disease (Matthew 10:1)." They were to use this power and to expect demonstrations to take place as an extension of the ministry of Jesus Christ. Jesus Christ commissioned them to preach the same Kingdom message that he was preaching. "And as ye go, preach, saying, the kingdom of heaven is at hand (Matthew 10:7)." As a result of preaching the same message, they could expect the same miracles. "Heal the sick, cleanse the lepers, raise the dead, cast out devils (Matthew 10:8)."

At the end of his earthly ministry, Jesus Christ commissioned his disciples a second time. "Go ye into all the world and preach the gospel to every creature (Mark 16:15)." Again, not only did he empower them to preach but he inspired them to expect miracles, signs and wonders to happen. "These signs shall follow them that believe; in my name they shall cast out devils, they speak with new tongues...they shall lay hands on the sick and they shall recover (Mark 16:17-18)." The disciples of Jesus Christ followed his instructions and they experienced the results that they were expecting. "They went forth preaching everywhere. The Lord working with them, and confirming the word with signs following (Mark 16:20)."

The ministry of the apostles of Jesus Christ is continued in the Book of Acts. When the apostles preached, something always happened. Acts records the early history of the church. It is filled with people having expectations and miracles, signs and wonders taking place.

When You Preach Expect Something to Happen

The ministry of Jesus Christ is not over. His ministry continues in each of us who have accepted our call to ministry. We are to continue to preach the Gospel of Jesus Christ to those who do not know him. We are to continue to preach the Gospel of the Kingdom to those who do know him. If we preach the same Kingdom message that Jesus Christ preached, then we can expect the same things to happen in our ministry that happened in the ministry of Jesus Christ. If we teach the same Kingdom principles that Jesus Christ taught, then we can expect the same miracles, signs and wonders to follow.

A good message is composed of four things: education, application, inspiration and demonstration. Education is the part of the message that teaches people something that they may not have known or reviews a principle that they may have forgotten. Application is the part of the message that takes the text off of the pages and applies it to real life situations that people can relate to. Inspiration is the part of the message that empowers people to do something with the Word that they have heard. Through inspiration, people are challenged to grow and change. Demonstration is the part of the message that shows the manifestation of the power of God right before their eyes before they leave the sanctuary. Some examples of demonstration are salvation, healing and deliverance.

Lack of expectation often produces a lack of demonstration. The more we expect, the more will be demonstrated in our ministry. It can happen during the message, right after the message, the next day, the next week, next month, next year, years down the road. "There shall be a performance of the things that were told you of the Lord (Luke 1:45)."

Questions for Reflection

1. How do you distinguish between a miracle, a sign and a wonder?

2. Give 5 examples of specific miracles, signs and wonders that followed the ministry of Jesus Christ. Please include scriptural references and do not repeat earlier used references.

    a.

    b.

    c.

    d.

    e.

3. Give 5 examples of specific miracles, signs and wonders that followed the ministry of the apostles of Jesus Christ. Please include scriptural references and do not repeat earlier used references.

    a.

    b.

    c.

    d.

    e.

4. Give examples of specific miracles, signs and wonders that follow your ministry.

5. What does the word, commission, mean?

6. Compare and contrast the disciples' first and second commission.

7. What does the word, gospel, mean?

Exercise Workspace

8. Compare and contrast the Gospel of Jesus Christ and the Gospel of the Kingdom.

9. Which definition of the Kingdom of God resonates most with you? Why?

10. Compare and contrast the miracle that took place through the ministry of Pastor Thompson to the miracle that took place through the early ministry of Minister Pulley.

11. What do you expect to happen when you preach and teach? Why?

12. List the 3 Revival Pointers that resonate with you the most and explain.

    a.

    b.

    c.

13. Which one of the 4 parts of a message are you most proficient in? Why?

14. Which one of the 4 parts of a message are you least proficient in? Why?

15. What can you do to become more proficient in the 4 aspects of a message?

Message #8a

Sermon Title: Make the people sit down – John 6:1-14

Sermon Type: Historical Incident

I. Introduction – Crowd Control

A. How do you organize a large group of people?

B. How do you ensure that everyone's needs are met?

C. Can you imagine being an usher at an event with over 15,000 people

1. 5000 men

2. 5000 wives (most men were married)

3. 5000 children (each couple had at least 1 child)}

II. Make

A. What a forceful word!

B. God is calling us to be radical and forceful not timid.

III. The People

A. You can't be effective in ministry if you don't want to deal with people.

B. People have issues.

C. People are hungry.

IV. Sit Down

A. Get a posture of expectancy, ready to receive.

B. Only those who sat down were feed.

V. Conclusion - You have what it takes to set things in order

A. In your home

B. On your job

C. In your community

D. With your church auxiliary.

Exercise

1. Give scriptural reference for each point of the message.

2. This message is organized by its title. Organize the 3 points of the message in different way.

3. Education - What five-fold ministry office is associated with order? How can you apply that concept of the message to teach people something that they may not have known?

4. Application - What part of this message is about life application?

5. Inspiration – What part of this message is about inspiration?

6. If you were preaching this message, what demonstration can be expected?

7. Add a hook to this message that would encourage people to come out the next night.

8. How can you add to this message the idea of inviting people to come to the revival?

Message #8b

Sermon Title: I put it all in his hands – John 14:1-13

Sermon Type: Historical Incident

I. Introduction – Hands are important part of the body. Explain the idea of putting something in someone's hands.

II. It does not matter what it is, put it in his hands – fish and bread

III. It does not matter how much or little you have, put it in his hands – 2 fish and 5 loaves of bread

IV. We can't experience a miracle until we put what we have in God's hands.

V. Conclusion – Song – "All in his hands, I put it all in his hands. This and that, I put it all in his hands!" What do you need to put in God's hands? Who do you need to put in God's hands?

Exercise

1. Add a review component to the outline which reviews the previous message.

2. What other song could be used to complement this message as a conclusion?

3. Do you use songs at the beginning, middle or end of your message? Why or why not?

4. Add information to the outline to develop the idea of the hands.

5. Add information to the outline to develop the fish and bread concept.

6. What is the biblical significance of the number, two? Add the information to the outline.

7. What is the biblical significance of the number, five? Add the information to the outline.

8. What are some practical ways that we can put things into God's hands? Add to the outline.

9. What are some practical examples of how we take things out of God's hands? Add to the outline.

Message #8c

Sermon Title: More than enough – John 14:1-13

Sermon Type: Historical Incident

I. Introduction – We settle for just enough to get by. Mediocre. Average. Just enough to pass.

II. God is able to use what you have if you put it in his hands – 2 fish and 5 loaves of bread

III. God is able to multiply what you have to meet the need – 5000 men + women and children

IV. God is able to give you increase, abundance, overflow, more than enough – 12 baskets of fragments.

V. Conclusion – 12 baskets, 12 preachers. Each preacher who served others experienced more than enough.

Exercise

1. Add a review component of the previous two messages for those who only came the last night.
2. What practical thing could you do while preaching this message that would help paint the picture of the story of the text? Be creative.
3. What is the biblical meaning of the number, twelve?
4. Give 5 practical examples of how people can experience more than enough in their lives.
5. Give an example of how you have experienced more than enough in your life.
6. Why do you think that only the men were actually counted and not the women and the children?
7. What is a fragment?
8. Develop the concept of fragment and add it to the outline.
9. Arrange the messages in order of your favorite (1-3) and explain why you placed them in that order.
10. Case Study: The revival was Wednesday, Thursday and Friday night. There were so many demonstrations at the revival and the people are so excited that the pastor of the church asked you to stay over and preach Sunday morning. Develop a message outline that complements the other 3 messages that you preached. You can use the same text or a different text.

Exercise Workspace

Exercise Workspace

Exercise Workspace

Exercise Workspace

CHAPTER NINE

THE Preacher's WRITINGS

(Age 15)

"If God told you something, you should write it down."
Pastor Ann Smith

Write on a scroll that which you see and read it to the seven churches.
Revelation 1:11

CHAPTER NINE—The Preacher's WRITINGS

After over 30 years of preaching and 20 years of pastoral ministry, Pastor Thompson made her transition from this dimension of life to the next. Shortly after Pastor Thompson's transition, I was molested by a 27-year-old choir director of one of the churches with whom we fellowshipped. Instead of recognizing it for what it was, molestation, they considered it fornication because I was a preacher. No consideration was given to the fact that I was a 15-year-old virgin. They focused solely on the idea that I was a minister and that I knew better.

I was not given an opportunity to share my side of the story. They were not interested in hearing about me being innocent. I was only asked three questions. The first question was "Did you go to his house?" My answer was "Yes, to get a tape for choir rehearsal." I was the director of the Youth Choir and I opened each rehearsal with a playback of our last performance. During the fellowship service between the two churches, Holy Name and his church, my cassette tape got caught in the tape recorder and I was unable to record the service. I knew he recorded the service as well, so I asked him to make me a copy of the tape. He agreed and when I went to his house to pick up the tape, he molested me.

The second question was "Did he take off his clothes." I said, "Yes!" The third question was "Did you immediately leave when he took his clothes off?" My response was "No!" I was so shocked when he began to take off his clothes that my entire body froze. I was unable to move. I was in a state of shock. I did not know what part of the conversation I had missed. I did not understand what I said or did to cause him to take off his clothes or mine. He masturbated, and I left his home in a daze wondering what had happened.

I was unable to shake the feeling of bewilderment, so I decided that it was my fault. My teenage brained concluded that I must have done something or said something that caused the entire experience, so I wrote him a letter of apology and mailed it to his house. He never received my letter. He lived with his aunt and uncle. His aunt intercepted my letter. She said, "The Lord Jesus told me to open that letter."

My letter became the evidence that they had been looking for, for years to prove that he was a homosexual and to have him excommunicated from the church. Although there was a 12-year age gap, the church considered me a fornicator because I was a preacher. The fact that I was a child and he was an adult seemed inconsequential.

My consequence for this perceived "sin" was being silenced for six months. I was unable to preach or teach Sunday School. I had to sit in the back of the church on the last row. I was not allowed to participate in the service in any way. I could not so much as clap my hands or pat my feet. The people in the church were also unable to speak to me before, during or after service. I was shunned.

All of my preaching engagements were cancelled by the church secretary. Letters were sent to all the churches that we fellowshipped with and to all the pastors in the counsel urging them not to let me preach in their churches. A copy of my letter to him was also attached. The pastors did not keep the situation confidential, I was the talk of the town.

I was devastated, depressed and suicidal. Being unable to preach was like taking the breath out of my body. I saw no reason to live and I was not motivated to do anything. I went to school, came home, ate a little and went to bed. I was a sophomore in high school and my grades suffered tremendously. I went from an honor roll student to barely passing.

In addition to being unable to preach, the most hurtful thing about being silenced is that my best friend, Darnell Foster, was getting married and I was unable to be the best man in his wedding. The belief was that the wedding had to be pure and a "fornicator" being a part of the ceremony would defile the holy matrimony.

My mother and my grandmother had entirely different perspectives. Like Job's friends, my mother, a babe in Christ and new to church politics, felt that I should just confess my sins and repent (Job 8). My grandmother felt that the entire church (including my mom) was crazy and that we should press charges against the man who molested her grandson. I begged my grandmother not go to Child Protective Services and not to get a lawyer. I did not desire any additional embarrassment or shame. I just wanted to serve my 6-month sentence and be done with the whole situation.

My grandmother was relentless so I prayed and asked God what to do. My internal guidance was to find him and to plead with him to tell the church officials the truth; I was innocent. His family did not speak to me or give me any clue as to where he was. They saw me as the person who got him expelled from the church. I went to his job only to find out that he quit. My next thought was to go to gay clubs, bars and any other place where I thought he might be.

After weeks of searching, I finally found him in a bar and he agreed to come to the Pastors' Council Meeting and tell them the truth. I will never forget that fifth Saturday in April when he showed up and I was vindicated. The pastors gave me a personal apology, but it paled in comparison to the rebuke and the shame that I experienced. No public apology was given to the churches. No new letter was sent to the pastors. I was just reinstated as a minister.

Out of thirteen pastors, there was one pastor in the Pastors' Council Meeting, Pastor Gladys Hairston, who fought for me and felt that an injustice had been done. She urged the clergy not just to reinstate me but to vindicate me. She reminded me of Pastor Thompson and I felt a divine connection to her. I left Holy Name Church of Jesus and joined Bible Revival Deliverance Church where she was the senior pastor.

Although Bible Revival and Holy Name shared the same denomination of the Apostolic Church, they were totally different. Bible Revival had a pastoral team of three dynamic women: Pastor Gladys Hairston who was the Senior Pastor, Pastor Ann Smith who was the Assistant Pastor and Dr. Bernice Edwell who was the Second Assistant Pastor. Bible Revival was also a deliverance ministry where miracles, signs and wonders took place almost every service. It was a highly spirited church and services lasted a lot longer because of all the dancing and shouting. It was nothing for a Bible Study to turn into a deliverance service or for a service to take place without any preaching because "the anointing was so high."

When I joined the church, I quickly gravitated to Pastor Ann Smith. I became her secretary and she became my mentor. Pastor Smith received a lot of engagements and preached a lot of revivals. I scheduled her engagements and traveled with her wherever she preached. I mailed her confirmation letters and handled the details of the engagements. Although the secretarial work was not directly related to preaching, it was through working with her on a daily basis and talking to her in reference to the engagements that I was able to receive impartation from her that a lot of the other ministers did not receive. I loved Pastor Smith's preaching. Her preaching was always so creative and practical, yet thorough. I attribute a lot of my preaching style to Pastor Smith.

One of the greatest gifts that Pastor Smith gave me is the freedom to write. Under Pastor Thompson, preachers could only write down the subject of the message and the scripture reference. Everything else had to be remembered or spoken extemporaneously. There were so many times that I sat down from preaching thinking that I forgot to say this or I should have said that to make the message better.

Pastor Smith told me that writing was important. She felt like if God said something to her that it was worth writing down. Pastor Smith opened my mind to answer the question, "where would we be today if none of the people of the scriptures thought to write anything down?" Not only do I give Pastor Smith credit for a lot of my preaching style, I also attribute my ability to write to her. I am able to turn a lot of what I preach and teach into books because of the way that she taught me to outline my messages. I've been outlining messages for so long that I think of a message now in terms of an outline. I outline the chapters to all of my books before I write them. Once the outline is done all I have to go is back and fill in and develop the points.

She encouraged me with several writing pointers:

1. Keep paper and pen beside your bed so if you get a preaching idea through a dream or a vision, you can write it down. God reveals himself to you in dreams

and visions.

2. Take a pad to prayer so if God says something to you while you are praying, you can write it down. I later called this a "Rev Book." When God reveals himself to you in prayer, praise and worship, write down what God says.
3. As you drive the car or ride the bus, keep paper and pen with you so that if you get anything creative, you can write it down (bumper sticker, billboard, radio commercial, and television advertisement). God reveals himself to you in ordinary ways if you are looking for him.
4. If it's written down, then you can always go back and develop the message idea later. But if it's not written down, then you are likely to forget it.
5. Journal. Write down your thoughts and feelings. God reveals himself to you through the events of your life.
6. Take notes. When you are in Bible Class or listening to a message, write down key points. "What is the Spirit saying to you that the preacher is not saying?"
7. Write down your topic and brainstorm. Everything that comes to your mind about the subject, write it down.
8. Brainstorm the scriptures about your topic. Every scripture that comes to your mind about the subject, write it down.
9. "Preaching a message is like writing a letter. If you can write a letter then you can preach a message. A message has an introduction, a body and a conclusion." Most of the books in the Bible were letters.
10. Write an outline for your message. Organize your thoughts. Have a systematic way to present the information.
11. Don't rely on your notes but have them there. Know the message well enough to preach without notes. "If the wind blows your notes away, you should still be able to preach the message. If you leave your notes home, you should still be able to preach."
12. Highlight verses and points with different colors so that they can stick out when you are preaching. Use a highlighter or a pen that has various color inks.

In addition to writing pointers, she gave me several other preaching pointers:

1. Always be looking for a message. Always be open for God to speak to you, anytime, anywhere and through anybody to give you a message to give to God's people. "You are a messenger and you have a message for this age which is a

mess."

2. Always have a catchy title. Make people remember you and what you preached.
3. Go for shock and awe. Have people leaving the church saying, "I can't believe that he said...Can you believe that she said...?" There are so many preachers. "Preachers come a dime a dozen. You have to say and do something to make yourself stand out."
4. In the introduction, get the people's attention. Within the first three minutes people decide if they are going to listen to you or tune you out. Say something that people can relate to.
5. "Have three main points like an essay's thesis statement has three main points. If you have more than three points, people get bored. If you have less than three points, the message may not be meaty enough."
6. Don't be afraid to step out of the box and make people think. Look for a new way to present a familiar text.
7. Read the text several times. Each time, read it as if you never read it before. Don't assume that you know the story or the text.
8. Pay close attention to every detail of the text. "Get all that meat off the bones."
9. Once the message is written, get away from it for a day or two and then pick it back up and read it again.
10. Have a reservoir of messages on hold, just waiting to be preached. The Spirit will tell you who needs that message and where to preach it.

Questions for Reflection

1. Compare and contrast the mentoring that the young preacher received from Pastor Thompson to the mentoring he received from Pastor Smith. Give 3 comparisons.

   a.

   b.

   c.

2. Give 3 contrasts between Pastor Thompson and Pastor Smith as mentors.

   a.

   b.

   c.

3. Compare Holy Name Church of Jesus and Bible Revival Deliverance Church. Give 3 ways in which they were similar.

   a.

   b.

   c.

4. Contrast Holy Name and Bible Revival. (You may have to refer back to previous chapters to gather your information). Give 3 ways in which they were different.

   a.

   b.

   c.

5. List all the different churches that you have been a part of and describe the different things that you have received from each church/pastor that have developed you into the preacher that you are today.

Questions for Reflection (continued)

6. How can working closely with a pastor/mentor aid the development of a preacher?

7. What format do you use to write and organize your message (bullet points, outline, manuscript)? Why?

6. List the pros and cons of bullet points, outline and manuscript.

7. What is the most common way that you receive a message (prayer, life experience, another message)? Why?

8. Do you think messages that are read verbatim are effective? Why or why not?

9. Instead of pen and paper, what are some other ways that we can record what God is saying to us?

10. Do you think the introduction, 3 point and conclusion structure of a message is effective for you? Why or why not?

11. Are you always looking for a message? Why or why not?

12. How well do you know your messages before you preach them?

Questions for Reflection (continued)

13. What are some ways that you can become more familiar with the message before it is preached?

14. What do you feel was your most creative message? Why?

15. Are you comfortable going out on the limb and saying or doing something while preaching that is out of the ordinary? Why or why not?

16. Read Philemon, II John, III John and Jude. Choose 2 of them to outline in the format of introduction, body (3 points) and conclusion.

17. Which one of Pastor Smith's writing pointers resonates with you most? Why?

18. Which one of Pastor Smith's writing pointers resonates with you least? Why?

19. Which one of Pastor Smith's preaching pointers resonates with you most? Why?

20. Which one of Pastor Smith's preaching pointers resonates with you least? Why?

21. Compare and contrast Pulley's Preaching Pointers to Pastor Smith's Preaching Pointers. Give 3 comparisons.

    a.

Questions for Reflection (continued)

b.

c.

24. Give 3 contrasts between the two sets of Preaching Pointers.

    a.

    b.

    c.

25. List 5 ways that God may reveal himself to the preacher to get a message across.

    a.

    b.

    c.

    d.

    e.

Message #9

Sermon Title: Message - Jesus was not the only Christ - I Corinthians 10:1-4

Sermon Type: Topical

I. Introduction – What does Christ mean? Christ was not Jesus' last name. The anointing of God upon a person, place or thing to do something supernatural, beyond its natural or normal capabilities.

II. Christ was before Jesus. That rock was Christ.

III. Jesus was not born Christ. He developed and became Christ (Acts 2:36).

IV. Jesus was the Christ for his day (Acts 10:38). He healed the sick. He gave sight to the blind. He gave hearing to the deaf. He gave speech to the dumb. He walked on water. He feed 5000 with 2 fish and 5 loaves of bread. He cast out demons. He raised the dead.

V. Christ is after Jesus. Once Jesus Christ was resurrected, he became Christ Jesus and we become Christ in the earth today. Christ in you the hope of glory (Colossians 1:27).

VI. Conclusion - Everything that Jesus Christ was, we are. Now, we are the light of the world (John 9:5). Now, we are the salt of the earth (Matthew 5:13-16). Now, we are the living water.

Exercise

1. What was your first reaction to the title of the message? Why?

2. Give the message another creative and catchy title.

3. Give 5 biblical examples of Christ being a thing (such as the rock in the text) and add them to the outline.
   a. d.
   b. e.
   c.
4. Give 5 biblical examples of Christ being a person besides Jesus (such as the fourth person in the fiery furnace in Daniel 3) and add them to the outline.
   a. d.
   b. e.
   c.
5. Give 5 biblical examples of Christ being a place (such as the Red Sea in Exodus 13-15) and add them to the outline.
   a. d.
   b. e.
   c.
6. Give scriptural references for all the ways that Jesus demonstrated himself as Christ in point III of the outline.

7. Give 5 practical examples of how Christ in each of us can manifest himself and add them to the outline.
   a. d.
   b. e.
   c.
8. List 5 additional "I AMs of Christ," give scriptural references and describe in a sentence or two how you/we can be that today just as we are the salt of the earth and the light of the world.
   a. d.
   b. e.
   c.
9. How do you feel about being who Jesus Christ was in the earth today? How can you convey that through this message?

10. How do you feel about saying about yourself what Jesus Christ said about himself? How can you convey that through this message?

11. How do you feel about your ability to do what Jesus Christ did? How can you convey that through this message?

12. How do you feel about the capacity to do even greater works than Jesus Christ did (John 14:12)? How can you convey that through this message?

Exercise Workspace

CHAPTER TEN

Building the Preacher's CONFIDENCE

(Age 16)

"You can preach in front of anybody."
Pastor Ann Smith

Being confident of this very thing, that he which hath begun a good work in you will perform it until the day of Jesus Christ
Philippians 1:6

CHAPTER TEN—Building the Preacher's CONFIDENCE

Bible Revival was a member of an international organization, Pentecostal Churches of the Apostolic Faith (P.C.A.F.). Based on our location, we were a part of the Eastern and Southern States Council which held quarterly Council Meetings. The Council meetings were held the week leading to the Fifth Sunday of each quarter of the year. During Council Meetings, there were prayer meetings, business meetings and Bible Classes during the day and preaching at night. Saturday Night was Youth Night and they invited the young preachers to speak for a Platform Service. A Platform Service is a service where several preachers preach for about 5-10 minutes and there is no honorarium.

I was so nervous. This was my first time preaching live to an audience other than my local assembly or a church in which I was invited as the guest speaker. During the Council Meeting, there were going to be bishops, district elders (overseers), pastors (set gifts), elders and preachers from all over the Council (diocese) present. My palms were sweaty. My heart was beating so fast that I thought it was going to jump out of my chest. My stomach was doing summer saults and I could not stop going to the bathroom.

On one of my trips to the bathroom, I saw my mentor, Pastor Ann Smith, and she told me to calm down. She said, "Picture all the dignitaries in their underwear or sitting on the toilet. They are all human and men just like you who put their pants on just as you do. God has given you a message and you can preach it in front of anybody even the President of the United States of America." Needless to say, it made me laugh and calmed me down.

The message turned out very well. I preached about being delivered from public opinion. It was very effective. It's amazing that the Word was about worrying about what people think about us and that was the exact thing that was making me so nervous. I was overly concerned about what the dignitaries would think about me and my preaching.

What Pastor Smith said empowered me to get through the service until it was my turn to preach. As soon as I put the microphone in my hand and started talking, the nervousness left. To this day, I preach with a microphone in my hand. I don't use lavaliere, lapel or hand-set microphones. For me, I feel most comfortable holding the microphone in my hand. No matter how nervousness I feel as soon as I put the microphone in my hand, I feel empowered.

According to Pastor Smith, it is important that preachers balance their nervousness. Later on in the week, she later told me, "A little nervousness is good. If you don't have a little anxiety, then it means that you are in flesh or operating in ego. You are not relying on the Spirit. Too much nervousness is not good. You don't want to be so nervous that you can't do your job but you don't want to be so confident that you can't hear from God."

Confidence Builders

1. *Know your message like you know your name.* Read and re-read the text. Review your notes. The better you know your message, the less anxious you feel.
2. *Preach the message to yourself.* Preach the message in the mirror. The word that you preach is first to you, then to everyone else.
3. *Preach to the atmosphere.* The atmosphere carries the Word that you preach. "So shall my word be that goes forth out of my mouth: it shall not return unto me void, but it shall accomplish that which I please, and it shall prosper in the thing whereto I sent it (Isaiah 55:11)." It is important to set the right atmosphere before the Word goes forth. No matter how great your message is, if the atmosphere is not ready to carry the message, then the message is not as effective. That's why several churches have a sermonic selection before the preacher preaches to set the atmosphere.
4. *Practice the message with family members and close friends.* The more you practice the message, the less nervous you feel. I grew up playing church. I played church with my cousins. After every service we would come home and mock the people in church. I played church in my community. I would always say, "Let's play church and I will be the preacher." Before I started playing church, I would preach in front of my teddy bears and action figures like GI Joes and Incredible Hulk.
5. *Visualization.* See yourself preaching and the message going over well. If I was going to an unfamiliar place to preach, then I would visit the church prior to preaching there to get a feel for the church. I still get nervous when I am preaching some place for the first time. With modern technology, I go on line to see the church. I may even watch a clip of the pastor preaching in the church.

On the Spot Anxiety Reducers

If you still feel nervous, when you get to the microphone, podium or pulpit, then try one of the following techniques:

1. **Sing a song** – if you can sing, sing a song. Allow this talent to help you in your preaching. Use the song to connect with the audience. Use the song to calm you down.
2. **Say a prayer** – Prayer gives you an opportunity to close your eyes, to go within and focus on God and not the people.

3. **Tell a joke** – If you are a comedian or people regard you as funny, tell a joke. Allow your gift of laughter to aid you into the preaching moment. Sometimes a joke can break the ice.
4. **Find a supporter in the audience** - Focus on a person in the audience that you know has your back and is with you and who will cheer you on. It can be a family member or friend.
5. **Meditation & Deep Breathing Exercises** – lead the congregation in a brief meditation telling them to focus on their breath. As you breathe deeply and get in touch with the Holy Spirit within, you will feel yourself calming down.

Confidence Blockers

One of the major confidence blockers is **worrying about what people think about you and the message that you are delivering.** We are messengers and we are only delivering the message. The mail carrier does not care about what you think about him or her. They only have one job and that is to deliver the mail. We may not like the contents of the mail especially if it's a bill or turn off notice. We may jump for joy once we receive the mail as we do if it's a check or a wedding invitation. However we receive the mail/messenger, it does not impact the mail carrier.

Contrary to popular belief, I am a shy person. I don't like speaking in front of people. I am not an orator or a public speaker. I don't have the gift of gab. I am not good with extemporaneous speeches. I am a preacher and what gives me the confidence to stand in front of people and preach is that I have a message from God that must be delivered. I am bold and strong when I preach because I'm saying what God told me to say—nothing more, nothing less and nothing else.

Another major confidence blocker is **comparing yourself to other preachers.** Admire other preachers, but avoid comparing yourself to them. Accept your own unique style. I used to have a preacher friend who did powerful crescendos every time he preached. His preaching was like watching a good movie with the plot, suspense and climax. He would start off his messages very slow. His voice would be so low that you barely heard what he was saying during the introduction to the message. Everyone had to be quiet to listen carefully to what he was saying. Then he would build up speed slowly and increase volume methodically with every point. He could also sing very well. As he got to the conclusion, the organist would play behind him and they would modulate keys. It was like music to the ears. By the end of the message, everyone would be standing on their feet, shouting and wanting more.

I tried a few times to preach like my friend. It never worked for me. First of all, I could not sing. Secondly, I was too excited about what I was preaching to have just one crescendo. In any one message, I have at least four crescendos: a crescendo for point one, another crescendo for point two, a third crescendo for point three and a grand finale crescendo during the conclusion. I had to accept my preaching style and do what worked for me.

Early on in my ministry, I watched television evangelists. I loved the way that they articulated and never broke a sweat. I wanted to be like them. I was tired of sweating out my clothes and being hoarse on Monday mornings. I thought to myself I can talk instead of hollering. I can stay calm instead of getting excited. I decided to stop wearing robes and African attired when I preached. Instead, I wore my suits like the people on television. I also tried giving out handouts. No matter how much I tried to stay calm, it didn't work. I would get excited and my tone and pitch would increase and then I would start sweating. I have ruined several of my good suits trying to be like other preachers. The handouts did not help me stay calm either. All it did was help the people follow what I was saying and caused them to get excited right along with me.

Finally, I learned to accept myself as a preacher. I learned to accept my unique style. I learned to do what worked for me. I was only effective when I was being myself and saying what God told me to say to the best of my ability. The added pressure of trying to mimic someone else's style only made me more nervous instead of confident.

Trying to mimic someone's style is like trying to fight using someone else's armor. Saul offered David his armor and weapons to fight Goliath. David tried them on but he felt uncomfortable (I Samuel 17:38-40). Eventually, David realized that he could not fight the giant in someone's equipment. David accepted himself as a warrior. He remembered the success that he had with the lion and the bear when he was fighting the way that he knew how—with his sling shot and the stones. We can only be successful when we are authentic. We can only be effective when we accept our unique style.

Questions for Reflection

1. Do you think the visuals that Pastor Smith gave the young preacher were appropriate? Why or why not?
2. What other visual can be used to ease tension and build confidence?
3. Which Confidence Builder resonates with you the most? Why?
4. Which Confidence Builder resonates with you the least? Why?
5. Which On the Spot Anxiety Reducer resonates with you the most? Why?
6. Which On the Spot Anxiety Reducer resonates with you the least? Why?
7. Do you worry about what the audience thinks about you and your message? Why or why not?
8. Do you compare yourself to other preachers? Why or why not?
9. What is balanced nervousness?
10. Are there times when you are more nervous than others? Why or why not?
11. Are there certain people that you are afraid to preach in front of? Why or why not?
12. Read the story of David and Goliath. List and describe 5 ways in which David exhibited confidence.

a.

b.

c.

d.

e.

Message #10

Sermon Title: The Greatest Deliverance – Galatians 1:6-10

Sermon Type: Textual

I. Introduction – God is able to deliver us from anything. We have witnesses of people here who have been delivered from various things. When I get to what God has delivered, you from give God praise.

II. God delivers people from various addictions (alcohol, drugs, gambling, shopping or smoking). The greatest deliverance in the church today is not the deliverance from addictions.

III. God delivers people from various sexual sins (fornication, adultery, pornography, orgies). The greatest deliverance in the church today is not the deliverance from sexual sins.

IV. God delivers people from various sicknesses, pains and diseases. The greatest deliverance in the church today is not healing from physical conditions.

V. Conclusion – The greatest deliverance in the church today is the deliverance from public opinion. We are still in bondage to what people think about us, say about us and do to us. If you can get delivered from people, you can be totally free to fulfill the purpose that God has for your life. Paul was writing to the church at Galatia.

Exercise

1. This is message of mysterious. You don't know what the greatest deliverance is until the end of the message. Have you ever preached a message were people did not fully understand the title until the end? Why or why not?

2. What do you think the "mysterious" style of this message?

3. At what point do you think that the scripture should be read in this message? Why?

4. Give a biblical definition of deliverance.

5. Define deliverance in your own words.

6. Do not assume that people in your audience know what you are talking about. How and where can a definition fit into this message?

7. List and explain 5 scriptures that speak of the word, deliverance.

8. List and explain 5 examples in scripture where God actually delivers his people or a particular person.

9. From each of the points in the message, give a personal example of being delivered or helping someone be delivered.

10. Do you think that deliverance from public opinion is the greatest deliverance? Why or why not?

Exercise Workspace

Exercise Workspace

CHAPTER ELEVEN

THE Preacher and the Altar

(Age 17)

"After you preach, the anointing is on you to minister
to the people at the altar."
Dr. Bernice Edwell

The Spirit of the Lord is upon me, because he hath anointed me to preach the gospel to the poor; he hath sent me to heal the brokenhearted, to preach deliverance to the captives, and recovering of sight to the blind, to set at liberty them that are bruised, to preach the acceptable year of the Lord.
Luke 4:18-19

CHAPTER ELEVEN—THE Preacher and the Altar

Bible Revival had a three-fold chord of leadership. Pastor Gladys Hairston was the Senior Pastor. Pastor Ann Smith, my mentor, was the Assistant Pastor and Dr. Bernice Edwell was the Second Assistant Pastor. Although, I was not as close to Dr. Edwell as I was to Pastor Smith, I learned a lot just by watching Dr. Edwell. Dr. Edwell inspired me in a lot of ways:

1. She was the first person in my denomination to have a doctorate degree.
2. She had her own radio broadcast.
3. She established a School of Ministry at Bible Revival with curriculum, tracks and degrees.
4. She had a heart for evangelism and community outreach.
5. She knew how to make an altar call and how to minister to people at the altar.

When I first came to Bible Revival, all I wanted to do was preach and sit down afterwards because that is the way that I was taught in my previous churches. Just like giving the invocation and reading the scripture, preaching and doing the altar call were two different parts of the program performed by two different ministers.

I felt that after I preached that someone else could do the altar call. Preaching to me was like cooking and I love to cook. I enjoy preparing, cooking and serving people delicious meals. I like people to enjoy the food that I prepare. However, after I have worked in the kitchen, I want someone else to wash, dry, and put away the dishes. I feel like someone else can put away the food, clean the counters as well as sweep and mop the floor.

Through Dr. Edwell, I learned that while the Word is being preached, people make a connection with the preacher and the message that is shared. Although we are preaching to the general audience, people personalize the message and make individual application of the message right while the message is being preached. I can't tell you how many times people have come up to me after a service and said one of the following statements:

1. "I don't know about anyone else but that message was just for me."
2. "God sent you here today for me. I needed to hear that."
3. "God had a special message for me and he sent you here to deliver it."
4. "I felt like you were preaching right to me as if no one else was here but me and you."
5. "There is no way that you could have known that unless God told you to say

that."

Not only do the people need to make connection with the preachers in order for the message to be effective, the preachers also need to make connection with the people. Dr. Edwell taught me that after we preach, it was just as important for us as preachers to make connection with the people individually. In some denominations, at the end of the service the preacher goes to the back of the local assembly and greets each person at the door. This allows the people to establish a one-on-one rapport with the preacher and to share with him or her how they were personally impacted by the message. It is also an opportunity for people to affirm the preacher and the message that was preached.

"The Spirit of the Lord God is upon me because he has anointed me to preach ... (Luke 4:18)." Since I was a little boy, I always knew that God had anointed me to preach. With all of my faults, failures and issues, I always had an assurance that God had chosen me to deliver messages to his people. With full knowledge of my identity, I was confident that had God anointed me. I understood that I didn't have to pretend to be someone else in order to be anointed. It was clear to me that God does not anoint any false selves and that pretense and hypocrisy detract from the anointing. I knew that God only anoints authenticity but I did not know that the same anointing that was upon me to preach was also upon me to do the altar call.

Dr. Edwell taught me that the anointing of God that was upon me when I preached did not lift off of me as soon as I finished preaching. She taught me that it was not only my responsibility to preach the message but it was also my duty as a preacher to make the altar call and to minister to the people at the altar.

The Altar

Biblically, the altar is a symbol of worship. Many Old Testament patriarchs (Noah, Abraham, Isaac, Jacob, Moses, David) built altars to represent their personal relationship with God. Jesus Christ also encouraged his disciples to bring their gifts to the altar (Matthew 5:23-24). As disciplined followers of Christ today, we also are called to the altar. The altar is more than just the front of the church or the place where the minister preaches or the place where people make wedding vows. The altar is the special place in God's house where we make covenant with God.

Often when I have typed the phrase, Altar Call, the computer would change the phrase to "Alter Call." After several experiences with autocorrect, I realized that the Altar Call is the time where lives are altered. It is during the Altar Call that people are altered for the rest of their lives.

The Altar Call

An Altar Call is the point in the worship experience where the preacher calls for people to make a decision about the message that they have heard. The Altar Call is a call for action. The scripture commands us to be "doers of the word, and not hearers only, deceiving your own selves (James 1:22)." The Altar Call is also the time where the message that is preached is confirmed through miracles, signs and wonders. Within one altar call, people are presented with five opportunities:

1. Salvation – the awakening of the consciousness to the Truth that we are God's children (Genesis 1:26, Acts 2:40, Romans 8:16, Philippians 2:12)
2. Prayer – agreement with the person about a specific request (Amos 3:3, Matthew 18:19, Philippians 4:6)
3. Healing – releasing the person from any sickness, pain or disease and affirming health and wholeness (Matthew 4:23, Mark 16:17-18, James 5:14)
4. Baptism – cleansing of the mind from error thinking and clearing the heart from any guilt, shame or condemnation and the infilling of the Holy Spirit (I Corinthians 12:13, Ephesians 4:5, Hebrews 10:22)
5. Membership – becoming a part of a spiritual community (Acts 2:47, Galatians 2:9)

When making the Altar Call, the preacher must be skilled at connecting the message to these five opportunities. It is also important for the preacher to be prepared to minister to the people who come to the altar.

Altar Call Pointers

Through working with Dr. Edwell at the altar, I learned several pointers about doing Altar Calls and ministering to people at the altar:

1. People come to the altar for different reasons. Don't assume you know why they are there; ask them. Make sure to address the reason that they came to the altar even if you discern that there are other things taking place in the person's life.
2. You can't do the altar call alone. Although you may say the words that lead people to the altar, allow other ministers whom you trust to assist you with ministering to people at the altar.
3. In addition to ministers at the altar, it is important to have trained altar workers there to assist you with the physical mechanics of the altar:
   a. Having tissues available for people who may be crying
   b. Assisting people with getting back to their seats or to another part of the

local assembly for continued prayer/ministry

c. Moving the prayer line along, especially if there are a lot of people at the altar

d. Referring people to different prayer chaplains.

4. Before people come to the altar, it is important to have prayer warriors sitting in their seats silently praying for people who may be struggling with making the decision to come to the altar.

5. Be careful how and where you touch people at the altar. When praying with people, holding their hands or slightly touching their shoulders are good ways to make contact with them.

6. If there is a person in the audience that does not come to the altar but you feel inspired to pray with the person, out of courtesy ask the person can you pray with him or her before you start praying.

7. If the Spirit gives you something to personally share with a person, be sure that the microphone is not near your mouth. Speak softly to the person in his or her ear so that others do not hear the personal message that you have for that person.

8. If there is a person at the altar that you do not know or do not feel comfortable with, introduce yourself to the person and allow the person to introduce themselves to you. There is nothing wrong with establishing a brief rapport with a person at the altar before you minister to that person.

9. Soft music can often set the atmosphere for the Altar Call.

10. A person's safety is most important at the altar. People have different experiences and backgrounds as it relates to Altar Calls; therefore, allow the altar workers to assist you with keeping everyone safe.

11. The ministers and altar workers who assist at the altar are to have their own needs (healing, prayer, etc.) meet first before they attempt to assist others at the altar.

12. If it is just impossible for you to do the Altar Call, due to fatigue or having another engagement, then pray for another minister who can carry out that part of the assignment.

13. There is nothing wrong with calling people to the altar and saying a general prayer for all the people who come to the altar. You may not be able to individually pray for each person.

14. Do not feel like the ministry at the altar was ineffective because you do not see an immediate response. Do not try to force a response that people are not ready for.
15. There is nothing wrong with educating people at the altar about what is happening or what they can expect to take place, especially if you notice that they are fearful or uncomfortable.

The Smoking Deacon

After I preached the message, "Development Takes Place in the Dark," a lot of people came to the altar for prayer. I was a guest speaker at this particular church and many of the people who came to the altar were people who were in leadership positions in that church. One of the people who came the altar for prayer was the Chairman of the Deacon Board. When I asked the deacon what was his prayer request, he did not say. He just said that he wanted prayer. While I was praying for the deacon, I saw a vision of a pack of Kool 100's Menthol cigarettes; therefore, I incorporated in my prayer that God would deliver him from smoking for the sake of his health. I made sure that I was not speaking in the microphone and I whispered this portion of the prayer in his ear so that his privacy was respected. I was so nervous because I did not see any visible signs of him being a smoker (lips, teeth, gums, finger tips, smell in his clothes) but I knew what I saw in the Spirit.

The deacon became irate and unseemly during the Altar Call. He yelled in the service so that all of the congregation could hear, "I don't smoke. I don't know why you would say that to me." In a calm soothing voice, I whispered to him, "Everything is alright just let God work in your life." The softer I spoke, the louder he became so much so that the entire service stopped and everyone was watching him and I as if it were a movie.

I asked the deacon if we could talk in the office. He refused. He yelled, "No, we are going to settle this right here and right now. You are not going to embarrass me." I asked him, "Are you sure that this is how you want to handle the situation in front of all of these people?" The deacon shouted, "Yeah!" With the pastor's permission, I agreed and I told him with full confidence and assurance that I knew that he was a smoker. He asked me how I could say that to him knowing his title and position in the church. I told him that all I knew is what God showed me. I told him the exact type of cigarettes that he smoked and as I was talking God also showed me him smoking in the shed at night. After I gave him this word of knowledge, he came back to the altar, got on his knees, repented and cried out for help. I ministered to him and he was delivered from cigarettes that day and reports that he never smoked again.

I learned several things from this experience:

1. You never know what to expect during an Altar Call.
2. Regardless of how people respond, follow proper protocol.

3. Even after you do everything right, people are still dealing with their own issues at the altar and may respond in various ways.
4. If God shows you something or tells you something, don't back down.
5. Trust the voice of God, despite appearances. No matter what it looks like or sounds like, stand on God's word. Hold your ground.
6. Leaders and ministers sometimes need to come to the altar, too.
7. Don't be intimated by people's titles and positions because we all have something in our lives that we are working on.

Questions for Reflection

1. What is an altar?
2. Give Bible references for the five biblical figures that built altars and briefly describe the circumstances under which those altars were built.
3. Compare and contrast the use of the altar in Genesis to its use in the Tabernacle.
4. Are there any differences between the altar in the Tabernacle and the altars in Temple? If so, explain them.
5. Compare and contrast the use of the altar in the Old Testament to its use in the New Testament.
6. Compare and contrast how Altar Calls were done at Holy Name Church of Jesus to how they were done at Bible Revival Deliverance Church?
7. Explain how and what the young preacher learned from Pastor Smith compared to what he learned from Dr. Edwell.
8. What can you do to be more authentic?

9. Describe a positive experience that you had at the altar.

10. Describe an experience at the altar that was not so pleasant.

11. How are Altar Calls conducted at your church?

12. What is the difference between a prayer chaplain and an altar worker?

13. Do you like doing Altar Calls? Why or why not?

14. Which one of the 5 opportunities at the altar are you most comfortable leading? Why?

15. Which one of the 5 opportunities at the altar are you least comfortable leading? Why?

16. Choose one of scriptural reference from each of the 5 opportunities and explain how it relates.

17. Which Altar Call Pointer resonates most with you? Why?

18. Which Altar Call Pointer resonates least with you? Why?

19. What are some other ways to handle the situation with "the Smoking Deacon"?

20. Are there any additional lessons that you feel can be learned from the "Smoking Deacon" situation that were not listed? If so, list them.

Message #11

Sermon Title: Development Takes Place in the Dark - Matthew 10:24-27

Sermon Type: Topical

I. Introduction – After God brings us out of the darkness of sin, God takes us into another darkness of development. Examples - a baby in the womb, pictures in a dark room, vegetables/plants that grow under ground.

II. Faith - Even though, you can't see what's happening in the dark, you have to trust that something is happening.

III. Patience – We can't rush into the light prematurely or we will destroy the picture or bring death to the baby or the plant will die.

IV. Adjustment – When you have been in darkness so long, you have to adjust to the light. Even at the proper time and full term labor, the baby's eyes still have to adjust to the light.

V. Conclusion – Grow in the Dark and glow in the dark. God is still in you in your dark places, dry places and wilderness experiences. You are not alone.

Exercise

1. What are some differences between the darkness of sin and the darkness of development? Incorporate them in the outline.

2. List any other natural examples of development in the dark.

3. Give scriptural references to accompany each of the points in the message. Explain why you chose that scripture.

4. What is the strongest point of the message? Why?

5. What is the weakest point of the message? How can you develop it to make it stronger?

6. Give a personal or biblical example of faith in the dark.

7. Give a personal or biblical example of patience in the dark.

8. Give a personal or biblical example of adjustment to the dark/light.

9. What is it about this message that you believe brought so many church leaders to the altar?

10. How do you think the "Smoking Deacon" connected personally to this message?

11. Offer a different conclusion of the message and explain why you chose to change it.

12. Write a paragraph describing what you would say to transition people from the message to the altar call.

Exercise Workspace

Exercise Workspace

CHAPTER TWELVE

THE Preacher's DISCRETION

(Age 18)

"Use discretion. Preach the Bible but not the whole Bible in one sermon."
Bishop Horace O. Ward

Behold, I send you forth as sheep in the midst of wolves:
be ye therefore wise as serpents, and harmless as doves.
Matthew 10:16

CHAPTER TWELVE—THE Preacher's DISCRETION

When I was a senior in high school, God gave me a vision of everything in my life being on or off of Liberty Road, one of the main streets in Baltimore. Liberty Road begins in the inner city of Baltimore and continues to suburbs of Baltimore County. In the vision, I was riding a bus and I kept getting on and off the bus at various stops. Each stop had a sign that identified a different aspect of my life: work, school, home and church.

The first stop was farthest north on Liberty Road on the right side of the street and it was labeled, "WORK." I understood that sign because I was a Pharmacy technician and cashier at Giant, a popular grocery store that was off of Liberty Road on the right-hand side of the street. Going south, the next stop also on the right-hand side of the street was labeled, "SCHOOL." That sign also made sense because my high school, Milford Mill Senior High School, was also off of Liberty Road. Continuing south was the third sign but it was on the left-hand side of the street and it was labeled, "HOME." I had no challenges with this sign either because my house on was off of Liberty Road and the home sign correlated with where I lived in proximity to the other signs. The fourth and final sign was the farthest south on the right side of the street and it said, "CHURCH." This sign did not make sense because my church, Bible Revival, was not off of Liberty Road. In fact, Bible Revival was all the way on the other side of town.

I meditated on the vision to get clarity about what I saw. I prayed and I asked God to give me an understanding of the fourth sign. I even shared the vision with my mentor, Pastor Ann Smith, to see if she had any insight. Pastor Smith said the only thing that she could interpret from the vision is that I was going to be a part of a church that was located off of Liberty Road. Neither she nor I liked that interpretation of the vision because we enjoyed working together in ministry.

Over the next few months, whenever Bible Revival was not having service, I visited churches on the southern part of Liberty Road that were located on the right side of the street. I only felt at home at one of the churches, Church of the Redeemed where the pastor was Bishop Horace O. Ward.

I continued to visit Church of the Redeemed alternating service days with Bible Revival's Schedule of Service. After visiting Church of the Redeemed for three months, it became crystal clear to me that it was the place that I saw in the vision. I knew in my heart that it was the church that I was called to for the next dimension of my life and ministry. It also called me to review what I had learned from my previous church experiences.

At Holy Name Church of the Jesus, under the auspices of Pastor Thompson, I learned the

Spiritual Disciplines of:

1. Prayer
2. Fasting
3. Reading and Studying the Scriptures
4. Praise & Worship
5. Stewardship (tithing my time, talents and treasure)
6. Fellowship with the saints
7. Witnessing to the lost and sharing my testimony with others

As it relates to ministry, I learned

1. To always be prepared to preach
2. To know your message well enough not to be dependent on my notes
3. To never preach for money but because you love God and you love to do it.
4. Being a minister was more than preaching but serving in various ministries in the church
5. To know the Bible well enough to not just preach it but to teach it
6. To expect something when I preached
7. To never be satisfied with where I was in preaching that I could always improve and get better
8. To preach a revival or take a theme and break it up over days

I also discovered and developed my gift of faith: I could believe God for anything and it would happen because I believed it.

At Bible Revival, I learned

1. Salvation, Healing and Deliverance
2. Miracles, Signs and Wonders
3. Impact of music in the service
4. Importance of education
5. Grace, mercy and forgiveness

As it relates to ministry, I learned

1. Preaching with notes (outlining my message, structure of the message, high-

lighting important points)

2. Always be open to preach look for a message
3. Confidence in my preaching
4. Altar Call and Altar Work
5. To be open to the flow of the Spirit
6. How to lift offerings

Leaving Bible Revival was not easy for me but it was important for me to leave properly. It is imperative that we as ministers, preachers, teachers, healers, spiritual leaders that we do things decently and in order, especially as it relates to making a transition in ministry (I Corinthians 14:40)." There is a right way and a wrong way to do anything. I treated my leaving Bible Revival that same way that I would leave a job that was paying me. I submitted my letter of resignation 30 days in advance because I was considered essential staff. I began finding potential replacements for all of the tasks that I was doing in the church (Men's Ministry, Assistant Choir Director, Administrative Assistant to the Assistant Pastor, etc.). My last service, I returned all keys and church property that was entrusted into my care. Whenever we are following the leading of the Holy Spirit to make a change, we have no problem with communicating the change and carrying it out .

Bible Revival was a much larger church in comparison to the church that was I was moving to, the Church of the Redeemed. Everything thing that I learned at Church of the Redeemed can be summarized in one word, discretion. I learned through positive examples and experiences what to do. I also learned through negative examples and experiences what not to do. Every person is our teacher; every experience is our lesson.

Discretion with Preaching

"Preach the word; be instant in season, out of season; reprove, rebuke, exhort with all long suffering and doctrine (I Timothy 4:12)*."*

At the Church of the Redeemed, I learned discretion about preaching. I learned not to be too long and not to be too short. If I were too long, then I would lose the people's attention. The average attention span for a person to sit in one setting and be totally engaged is about 20 minutes. I remember as a teacher, having to change my teaching modality every 15 minutes. I could not lecture for an entire class period. I lectured for 15 minutes. Then, I had a small group activity for 15 minutes. Finally, we had large group reporting and discussion for the last 15 minutes. Like my students in the classroom, we have a lot of people in our congregations who are challenged with ADD or ADHD and they can only listen for a short period of time. Therefore, we have to be clear, concise and engaging. The millennials tend to be an overly stimulated generation who is used to being entertained most of the day through video games, interactive television and constant short message communication such as text and instant messages.

I remember as a young preacher, preaching for an hour, an hour and a half and one time I even preached 2 hours. I might as well have been preaching to myself because people were not engaged. It was information overload. It was my ego trying to impress people with all that I knew and had studied. Preaching and teaching is never about impressing anyone; it is about giving a message that the Spirit has given us to share. Through my 30 minute weekly radio broadcast, Cross Ministries, I learned to shorten my messages. The introduction was 90 seconds; the outro was 30 seconds. So, my message could not be any longer than 28 minutes.

As a young minister, Bishop Ward gave me a tremendous gift. He encouraged me to start an early morning service. This gave me the opportunity to preach weekly at a consistent time and to develop a congregation. He was able to give me this gift because I was the only other minister in the church besides himself. Through the 8 AM service, my preaching and teaching went to the next dimension. I was really able to perfect my craft and develop my own style. Sometimes two or three would be gathered and other times there were more people in the 8 AM service than the 11 AM service. Nevertheless, it was not about the numbers it was about the opportunity to learn, grow and to receive consistent feedback.

The Holy Spirit gave me the theme, Faith, for the year. I used Hebrews 11 as my focus scripture and for a year we covered the heroes and heroines of faith. I encourage set gifts and spiritual leaders to develop a theme for the year that is broad enough to break it down for the month and/or the week. It can be challenging to receive direction for week-to-week messages.

I learned preaching discretion. I discovered that everything cannot be covered in one message. I learned that there is nothing wrong with having Part 2 of a message or picking up the next week where you left off the previous week. I discovered that there is nothing wrong with a monthly series. I also learned that it was alright to start a message in one place and finishing it another time in another place.

Discretion with Places

"You will be blessed when you come in and blessed when you go out (Deut. 28:6)."

Church of the Redeemed was considered liberal in comparison to the other churches of which I was a member. They had no issues with me attending school dances, proms and listening to secular music. I was also free to go to the movies, skating, bowling and contact sporting events. It was at the Church of the Redeemed that my childhood was redeemed. I was no longer just the little boy preacher. I was free to be a teenager who happened to be a preacher; therefore, I could go to my senior prom.

As a result of the religious beliefs at Bible Revival, I did not go to my junior ring dance. Due to my role as a minister, I denied myself and my family the junior prom experience. They did not get to see me ride off in the limousine in my tuxedo with my date because I was a preacher. Although I was a class officer who planned junior events for my classmates, I wasn't able to attend these events because the thinking at Bible Revival "it was not a good look for a minister to be at a secular event."

When I came to Church of the Redeemed, I made up in my mind that I was going to my senior class events. I was not going to miss any of my senior class activities such as Senior Inauguration dance, Farewell Parties, class trips and prom because of my title or position as a minister. The pastor and members of the Church of the Redeemed support me in these endeavors and helped me recover from any past guilt, shame or condemnation.

Through attending the senior class events, I learned that I was able to conduct myself as a minister anywhere that I went. It became clear to me that it wasn't denying myself the privileges that made me a minister but how I conducted myself once I was there. Through discretion, I discovered that I was able let my light shine wherever I was (Matthew 5:16).

Discretion with People

"And there shall be, like people, like priest (Hosea 4:9)."

I also learned discretion with friendships. It became clear to me that each friend required time, money and energy; therefore, I needed to carefully consider whom I called friend. I also discovered that I needed friends who were not preachers and who were not a part of my church. These friends were able to be neutral non-bias third parties who were able to give me a different perspective on various matters.

Because the Church of the Redeemed was an intimate family church, I learned discretion as it relates to dual relationships with family members. For much of my ministry, my mother and I attended the same church. She was my mother who was fully in charge at home but at church I was a minister and she was not. I discovered how to navigate between family members and church family. It became clear to me that family members were not to receive extra privileges or special treatment.

I was talking to Bishop Ward one day about dating a young lady in the church. His response was "even a dog knows not to eat and poop on the same plate." He encouraged me to keep my personal life private from my ministry. As a single young man, I learned to keep my dates separate from church business. Bishop Ward said, "every time you date someone or end a relationship the congregants don't need to know." Therefore, even though I fellowshipped with various parishioners and went to their homes for dinner, I used discretion. I was still on duty as a minister and only shared public information.

Discretion with Practices

"For, brethren, ye have been called unto liberty; only use not liberty for an occasion to the flesh, but by love serve one another (Galatians 5:13)."

As a senior in high school, I fully accepted my call to ministry. Different from what my father thought, I knew that this was not a phase that I was going through; therefore, I made up my mind that I was going to have fun being a preacher. Since I was going to be a preacher for the rest of my life, then I had to do it as me and I had to have fun doing it.

I learned that everyone had their own expectations of ministers and that I could not live up to all of them. I also discovered that my favorite pastimes (playing cards and dancing) were not popular among preachers. None of the preachers that I knew played cards such as: spades, bid whist, pinochle, etc. Also, it was not popular for ministers to listen to secular music, dance and go to dance clubs. Therefore, my discretion as it relates to practices was to:

1. Discover what were my own principles that I was going to practice as a preacher.
2. Be aware that people do have expectations of preachers that are above normal human behavior.
3. Consciously decide which expectations that I was going to live up to.
4. Consciously decide which expectations that I was not going to live up to.
5. Accept the consequences for meeting and not meeting expectations.

Discretion with Principles

"All things are lawful unto me, but all things are not expedient: all things are lawful for me, but I will not be brought under the power of any (I Corinthians 6:20)."

In addition to using discretion with preaching, places, people and practices, I also learned, at the Church of the Redeemed, discretion with principles; such as

1. Be consistent with giving tithes and offerings (Stewardship).
2. If the church made a special appeal, give whatever amount that they are requesting (Example)
3. Get my Spiritual Leader's permission to take an engagement. (Respect for authority).
4. In addition to committing to daily prayer, commit to Early Morning weekly prayer (Spiritual Disciplines).

5. Read the books that mentors recommend (Learning).
6. Be open and honest. Anything that I have to hide it is best not to do it. Anything that I had to be ashamed if people found out, do not do (Integrity).
7. Live a holistically healthy, balanced and well-rounded life (Proper diet and regular exercise).
8. Do not date people in the church (Ethics).
9. If I received two engagements for the same date and one is a larger church and another one is a smaller church, keep my word to the first church (Equality).
10. If I miss the mark, admit it and learn from it. I will not try to cover up or justify your mistakes. Learn from your mistakes and move on. Don't beat yourself up. You are not perfect. You are not always going to dot all of your "I's" and cross all your "T's" (Development).

Theme: A Year of Faith—52 Sermons from Hebrews 11

Week 1- Definition of Faith
Week 2 - Now Faith
Week 3 - Faith: A Good Report
Week 4 - Faith & Creation
Week 5 - The Faith of Abel
Week 6 - The Faith of Enoch
Week 7 - Faith: A Pleasing God
Week 8 - The Faith of Noah
Week 9 - The Faith of Abraham - Part I (Leaving his Homeland)
Week 10 -The Faith of Abraham - Part II (Stranger & Pilgrim)
Week 11 - The Faith of Abraham - Part III (Offering up Isaac)
Week 12 - The Faith of Sarah
Week 13 - The Faith of Isaac
Week 14 - The Faith of Jacob
Week 15 - Dying in Faith
Week 16 - Faith for the Promised Land
Week 17 - Faith for a Heavenly City
Week 18 - The Faith of Esau
Week 19 - The Faith of Joseph
Week 20 - The Faith of Ephraim
Week 21 - The Faith of Manasseh
Week 22 -The Faith of Moses - Part I (Youth)
Week 23 - The Faith of Moses - Part II (Young Man)
Week 24 - The Faith of Moses - Part III (Adult)
Week 25 - The Faith of Moses - Part IV (Passover)
Week 26 - Faith to Pass Through the Red Sea
Week 27 - Faith to Make the Walls Fall Down
Week 28 - The Faith of Rahab
Week 29 - The Faith of Gideon
Week 30 - The Faith of Barak
Week 31 - The Faith of Samson
Week 32 - The Faith of Jephthae
Week 33- The Faith of David - Part I
Week 34 - The Faith of David - Part II
Week 35 - The Faith of David - Part III
Week 36 - The Faith of Samuel
Week 37 - The Faith of the Prophets
Week 38 - Faith to Subdue Kingdoms
Week 39 - Faith to Work Righteous
Week 40- Faith to Obtain the Promise
Week 41 - Faith to Stop the Lion's Mouth
Week 42 - Faith to Quench the Fire
Week 43 - Faith to Escape
Week 44 - Faith to be Strong
Week 45 - Faith to Fight
Week 46 - Faith to Make Them Run
Week 47 - Faith to Raise the Dead
Week 48 - Faith to Endure the Torture, Persecution, Destitution
Week 49 - Faith for a Better Resurrection
Week 50 - Faith in the Prison and Stoning
Week 51 - Faith in Temptation
Week 52 - Wandering in Faith

Exercise

Week 1. ____________________
Week 2. ____________________
Week 3. ____________________
Week 4. ____________________
Week 5. ____________________
Week 6. ____________________
Week 7. ____________________
Week 8. ____________________
Week 9. ____________________
Week 10. ____________________
Week 11. ____________________
Week 12. ____________________
Week 13. ____________________
Week 14. ____________________
Week 15. ____________________
Week 16. ____________________
Week 17. ____________________
Week 18. ____________________
Week 19. ____________________
Week 20. ____________________
Week 21. ____________________
Week 22. ____________________
Week 23. ____________________
Week 24. ____________________
Week 25. ____________________
Week 26. ____________________
Week 27. ____________________
Week 28. ____________________
Week 29. ____________________
Week 30. ____________________
Week 31. ____________________
Week 32. ____________________
Week 33. ____________________
Week 34. ____________________
Week 35. ____________________
Week 36. ____________________
Week 37. ____________________
Week 38. ____________________
Week 39. ____________________
Week 40. ____________________
Week 41. ____________________
Week 42. ____________________
Week 43. ____________________
Week 44. ____________________
Week 45. ____________________
Week 46. ____________________
Week 47. ____________________
Week 48. ____________________
Week 49. ____________________
Week 50. ____________________
Week 51. ____________________
Week 52. ____________________

Questions for Reflection

1. What discretion did the young preacher learn as it relates to preaching?
2. What discretion have you learned as it relates to preaching?
3. What discretion did the young preacher learn as it relates to places?
4. What discretion have you learned as it relates to places?
5. What discretion did the young preacher learn as it relates to people?
6. What discretion have you learned as it relates to people?
7. What discretion did the young preacher learn as it relates to practices?
8. What discretion have you learned as it relates to practices?
9. What discretion did the young preacher learn as it relates to principles?
10. What discretion have you learned as it relates to principles?

Conclusion

In high school, I only applied to one school, Morehouse College in Atlanta, Georgia. I wore a button every day that said, "Be somebody. Be a Morehouse Man." Once I was accepted into Morehouse, my mom, my grandmother and I argued about majors. My mom encouraged me to major in Pre-Law and to become a lawyer "to make money to take care of you and your family." She felt that I should not be dependent a congregation for financial stability. On the other hand, my grandmother said, "I think that you should be a journalist because you have such a way with words." I told them that I desired to major in Religious Studies and Theology so that I was able to learn more about being a preacher. My grandmother supported my decision and said "if you are going to be a preacher, then I don't want you to be no jack leg preacher...get some formal education and a terminal degree."

I received a full scholarship to Morehouse as a Religious Studies and Theology major. When I arrived at college the first week in August, the housing for freshmen was overbooked. We stayed in hotels in the area until they were able to resolve the issue. Because I was an only child and we had no family in Atlanta, my mom said, "I will give you two weeks to get me a stable address and telephone number or you are coming back home."

Two weeks later, I was on a plane back to Baltimore. I had no clue was what I was going to do about my education. I shared with a high school friend, Demetria Newsome, my Morehouse experience. Demetria said, "The Director of the Honors Program at Morgan State University is a member of my church and I will tell him your situation." Within a week, I had full scholarship to Morgan including tuition, fees, room, board and books. All I had to do was show up to the Freshman Orientation, Dr. Clayton Stansbury had taken care of everything. The next day I went to the front of the registration line and all my classes were paid for and preselected. All there was left for me to do was get my books and move into Argonne Apartments on campus. My family members were all there to help me get settled in as I began the next leg of my journey as a preacher, formal theological training.

In less than year, I became the founding president of Alpha Nu Omega Fraternity, Inc. I was ordained as an elder in Bible Way Churches Worldwide and I established the Church of the Everlasting Kingdom, Inc. I learned that preaching as a minister and preaching as a Spiritual Leader were very different. With each elevation from minister to elder to Spiritual Leader to overseer to bishop, my preaching has gone to a greater dimension of proficiency. I continue to learn lessons that I AM determined to share with other preachers all over the earth.

I build consciousness everyday about preaching through the following scripture (timeless truth), denial (negating that which I don't desire) and affirmation (holding on to the truth that I do desire to manifest).

Scripture – "It is the spirt that quickens. The flesh profits nothing. The words that I speak, they are spirit and they are life (John 6:63)."

Denial – I release and I let go from my soul and my body any erroneous ideas or limited beliefs that my ministry is limited to a certain type of person, a certain place or a certain time.

Affirmation – There is a multi-million-dollar life-changing word in my mind, in my mouth and in my hands. It is changing millions of lives and impacting thousands of communities for the good. It is bringing millions of dollars to me, to my family and all those who are connected to me. God promised me the INCREASE of the 5, 50, 500, 5000 and the miracle buildings. I believe it and I receive it now.

Pulley's 30 Preaching Pointers

1. Pray and ask God what God wants to communicate to the people.
2. Pick a topic and a text of which you are familiar and understand.
3. Posture: stand up straight and give the audience eye-contact.
4. Protocol: acknowledge dignitaries ie. pastor, other clergy, chairperson, family members, friends and others who have come to support you.
5. Pronunciation: Be able to say all of the words in your message and text. Use a bible dictionary for phonetic spelling.
6. Positive: Have a positive approach and title. Avoid fussing and being argumentative.
7. Personal testimonies should only be used as they relate to the message. Avoid using person's names without permission unless it is public knowledge.
8. Projection – speak loud enough for the audience to hear you. Use the microphone properly.
9. Pace – avoid speaking to fast or too slow. Too fast people can't understand. Too slow people get bored.
10. Prompt – be on time for the service. Lateness can be a distraction for you, the Spiritual Leader and the audience.
11. Prepare – Use your notes to assist you but be familiar enough with your message to do it without your notes.
12. Preach to yourself (in the mirror). The message is first to you. Live or live up to what you preach.
13. Populate the atmosphere with your words. The atmosphere is the carrier of your message.
14. Practice – your sermon with your spouse, close family member and preacher friends. If an unchurched person can understand your message, then you know that it is clear.
15. Picture yourself in the setting where you will be ministering and doing a good job.
16. Praise & Worship or prayer (altar work) should be your conclusion. Have an intentional conclusion.
17. Points – what are the 3 main points of your sermon? Do the points begin with the same letter? Rhyme?
18. Purpose – what is the purpose of your message? Answer this question so that everything you say and do is in line with the purpose of the message.
19. Presentation – make sure that your appearance is not a hindrance to the message. Do not wear anything that is too tight, too revealing, too low, too light and too anything else.
20. Participation – give the audience the opportunity to participate in the message (reading, sharing with the neighbor, interactive activities).

Pulley's 30 Preaching Pointers

21. Provoke your audience to think. Say something of quality that can change their lives. Teach them something that they may not have heard or known.

22. Principles – provide your audience with Kingdom principles to live by. What is the underlying principle of this message?

23. Practical examples of the principles should be used so that the audience can identify with the message and apply it to their lives (relationships, finances, health, housing, transportation, career).

24. Promote – balance in your interpretation of the scriptures. Consider the culture, history, language.

25. Present – the essential data of the text (5 W's and 1 H). Don't assume that the audience knows anything!
    - A. Who is speaking?
    - B. What is being said?
    - C. When is it being said?
    - D. Where is it written and where does the story take place?
    - E. Why (what events and activities surround the text)?
    - F. How does this apply to my life?

26. Prick your audience's memory. What are you doing to make the message memorable?

27. Paint a picture through details so that the audience can feel like they are there at the time of the text.

28. Plagiarism – avoid plagiarism. Give people credit for their words and ideas. Say where you received your information.

29. Pay attention to your audience. Their body language will let you know if they are with you and if they understand what is being said.

30. Professionalism – you are a professional. Conduct yourself as one before, during and after the message as it relates to handling the business of ministry (acceptance and confirmation of engagements, agree on honorariums ahead of time, send tax forms and complete hospitality form with all of your requests including food/beverages, transportation and lodging preferences, special requests, etc.)

18 ANNIVER
THIS DAY
LOVE TO OUR PASTOR A

Exercise

1. List and explain 5 pointers that you have perfected.

2. List and explain 5 pointers that you have not perfected.

3. Incorporate Pulley's Preaching Pointers in 5 sermon evaluations.

4. List and describe the Pulley's Preaching Pointers that connect with each chapter of the book.

5. Organize Pulley's Preaching Pointers in an order that makes sense to you. Give the rationale for your ordering of the points.

Types of Messages

Aspect	Textual/ Expository	Topical	Biographical	Historical Inci-dent/Narrative
Definition				
Occasions				
Advantages				
Disadvantages				
Structure				
Examples				

Exercise

1. What type of message do you prefer? Why?

2. What type of message do you least prefer? Why?

3. Develop an original message for each type of message.

4. Present and be evaluated on an original message for each type of message.

5. Complete an evaluation form for each type of message.

Mind of Christ School of Ministry

Bishop Doral R. Pulley, Presiding Prelate

Sermon Evaluation Form

Speaker: ________________________________ Date: ______/ ______/ ______
Title: ___________________________________ Time: (Start) _____ (Stop) ______
Subject: ________________________________
Scripture References: ______________________ Total Pts: _____/100 points
Radio? __ Tape? __ TV? __ Internet? __ Live? __ Grade: _____

I. Content (What significant points were made?) {___/25 points}

II. Delivery (How was it said? Was it clear and understandable?) {___/25 points}

III. Usage of Time (Did they exceed overall time limits? Did they spend too much time or not enough time on each point/part?) {___/25 points}

IV. Creativity (Did they effectively use personal anecdotes [short stories], illustrations, etc. to help relay their message? Consider the style in which they ministered in terms of creativity.) {___/25 points}

General Comments:

Name of Evaluator: ________________________________
Signature of the Evaluator: ___________________________

Glossary of Popular Terms

1. Sermon -
2. Message -
3. Homily -
4. Exegesis -
5. Eisegesis -
6. Homiletics -
7. Theology -
8. Teaching -
9. Training -
10. Workshop -
11. Seminar -
12. Speaking -
13. Preaching -
14. Anointing -

About the Author | **Dr. Doral R. Pulley**

Dr. Doral Reginald Pulley celebrates 40 years in ministry and has worked almost every capacity of the Church. He has traveled across the country spreading the Word of God in an innovative manner that empowers people to change. He is known for his ability to effectively train church leaders and to stimulate holistic growth and development.

At an early age, Dr. Pulley became aware of his true identity as a son of God and demonstrated a love for God and church, which distinguished him from other children. He accepted his call to ministry at the age of seven and was licensed as a minister at 12. He has served several churches in the Baltimore-Washington Metropolitan area as assistant, associate and senior pastor.

In 1992, Dr. Pulley graduate Magna Cum Laude from Morgan with a Bachelor's of Arts in Religious Studies and Theology. He received his Masters of Science in Pastoral Counseling from Loyola College of Maryland in 1996 and his Certificate of Advanced Study in 2000. He graduate in May 2010 with a Doctorate of Ministry in Pastoral Psychology from Graduate Theological Foundation.

Dr. Pulley is certified as a mental health professional by the National Board of Professional Counselors and by the State of Maryland as a Licensed Clinical Professional Counselor. After 20 years of service, he retired from being the Assistant Principal of St. Frances Academy, an inner city Catholic high school.

Dr. Pulley is the author of several books and publications including: *The Life Model for Spiritual Direction, A Guide to Establishing Mental Health Ministries; Redefining Relationships for the 21st Century; and It's Just That Simple: Love God, Love Yourself, Love Everyone Else.*

Dr. Pulley is the President and CEO of the Church of the Everlasting Kingdom, and network of local assemblies, ministries and businesses throughout the United States who manifest the Kingdom of God right here on earth.

Dr. Pulley was introduced to New Thought Christianity in 1996. Under the auspices of the Rev. Dr. Mary A. Tumpkin in 2009, he decided to further his metaphysical studies. In 2014 he graduated from the Johnnie Coleman Theological Seminary's Previously Ordained Clergy Program and received credentials from the Universal Foundation for Better Living, an international association of New Thought Christian churches, organizations, centers and study groups dedicated to spreading the abundant life teachings of Jesus Christ.

In August 2014, Dr. Pulley relocated to St. Petersburg, Florida and became the Spiritual

Leader of Unity of Midtown. The church has experienced phenomenal spiritual, numerical and financial growth under his leadership. In April 2017, Dr. Pulley expanded his ministry in the Tampa Area by establishing Today's Church, an all-accepting, Bible-based, Christ-centered Church who meets the diversified needs of today's people. In addition to pastoring, preaching, teaching, counseling, and writing, Dr. Pulley is the proud father of two beautiful twin daughters, Brittney and Courtney; one very successful son, D. Reginald, II and one granddaughter, Tyler Jade.

For speaking engagements or to order any of his publications, visit his website, www.doctorpulley.com.